The Digital Reader

Using E-books in K–12 Education

Terence W. Cavanaugh

International Society for Technology in Education

EUGENE, OREGON • WASHINGTON, DC

The **Digital Reader**
Using E-books in K–12 Education

Terence W. Cavanaugh

Director of Publishing
Jean Marie Hall

Copy Editor
Lynne Ertle

Acquisitions Editor
Scott Harter

Cover and Book Design
Signe Landin

Production Editor
Tracy Cozzens

Layout and Production
Kim McGovern

Production Coordinator
Amy Miller

International Society for Technology in Education (ISTE)
Washington, DC, Office:
   1710 Rhode Island Ave. NW, Suite 900, Washington, DC 20036-3132

Eugene, Oregon, Office:
   175 West Broadway, Suite 300, Eugene, OR 97401–3003
Order Desk: 1.800.336.5191
Order Fax: 1.541.302.3778
Customer Service: orders@iste.org
Book Publishing: books@iste.org
Rights and Permissions: permissions@iste.org
Web: www.iste.org

First Edition
ISBN 978-1-56484-221-3

About ISTE

The International Society for Technology in Education (ISTE) is a nonprofit professional organization with a worldwide membership of leaders in education technology. We are dedicated to promoting appropriate uses of technology to support and improve learning, teaching, and administration in PK–12 and teacher education. As part of that mission, ISTE provides high-quality and timely information, services, and materials, such as this book.

ISTE Book Publishing works with experienced educators to develop and produce practical resources for classroom teachers, teacher educators, and technology leaders. Every manuscript we select for publication is carefully peer-reviewed and professionally edited. We look for content that emphasizes the effective use of technology where it can make a difference—increasing the productivity of teachers and administrators; helping students with unique learning styles, abilities, or backgrounds; collecting and using data for decision making at the school and district levels; and creating dynamic, project-based learning environments that engage 21st-century learners. We value your feedback on this book and other ISTE products. E-mail us at **books@iste.org**.

ISTE is home of the National Educational Technology Standards (NETS) Project, the National Educational Computing Conference (NECC), and the National Center for Preparing Tomorrow's Teachers to Use Technology (NCPT3). To find out more about these and other ISTE initiatives and to view our complete book list or request a print catalog, visit our Web site at **www.iste.org**. You'll find information about:

- ISTE, our mission, and our members
- Membership opportunities and services
- Online communities and special interest groups (SIGs)
- Professional development services
- Research and evaluation services
- Educator resources
- ISTE's National Educational Technology Standards (NETS) for Students, Teachers, and Administrators
- *Learning & Leading with Technology* magazine
- *Journal of Research on Technology in Education*

About the Author

Terence W. Cavanaugh, PhD, is a visiting assistant professor in curriculum and instruction at the University of North Florida. He has degrees in science education and instructional technology, and his areas of research include curriculum design, assistive technology, and teacher education. As a university educator he instructs teachers in instructional technology, assistive technology, and educational design. Previous to his university work, he was a classroom teacher of Grades 6–12 for more than 15 years. Cavanaugh has taught science and technology in the United States, the Caribbean, Central America, and the Middle East. He has also worked as an educational consultant in reading technology, science, English for speakers of other languages (ESOL), exceptional student education, educational technology program development, and educational technology for school districts, the U.S. Department of Energy, colleges, and industry. The educational materials he has developed include books and Web sites on integrating media into science education, using electronic text in classrooms, integrating technology into curricula, and teaching learners with special needs.

Dedication

A good while ago, when I was just a boy in seventh grade, I discovered books. I say "discovered" because while I had been aware of books (going to the Tappin Book Mine almost every day), I discovered that books had the ability to take me places and show me things that I hadn't even imagined. It was at this time that I found a true love in books. So this book is dedicated to all those books (and authors) who helped shape my life: thank you. Oh, and Mr. Tappin, thank you, too!

Acknowledgment

My thanks, thoughts, and appreciation go to Cathy, my first reader and editor, for all her help, assistance, and patience as I worked on this project. Without your valuable contribution, this book could never have been written.

Contents

Part 2 Educational Applications Using E-books in the Classroom 35

Chapter 4 E-books Across the Curriculum 37

Chapter 5 E-book Reading Strategies 57

Introduction

The Promise of E-books

> **"** The Internet is the world's largest library. **"**

A book is a book is a book. However, we have reached a time in technology development when it is becoming harder to recognize a "book" right away. Recently while presenting a professional development session to a group of media specialists at a state reading conference, I asked them to define the word *book*. Most answers focused on an item made of a number of pages (made of paper) with words on them. When I showed them a book on tape, I asked whether it was a book. They all agreed that it was, so I showed them a child's CD storybook, *Arthur's Teacher Trouble*, and asked whether it was a book. Again, they agreed that it was. So then I showed my handheld computer running a program and put forth the same question. They weren't sure. I looked up *book* in several dictionaries and found the following definitions.

American Heritage Dictionary (online)
Book: NOUN 1. Set of written, printed, or blank pages fastened along one side and encased between protective covers. 2a. A printed or written literary work. (Houghton Mifflin, 2000)

Encarta Pocket English Dictionary
Book (n) 1. Bound collection of pages. 2. Published work. 3. Bound set of blank pages. 4. Set of things bound together. 5. Division of literary work. 6. Set of rules. 7. Bookmaker's record. 8. Script or libretto. 9. Number of tricks needed in scoring. 10. Imaginary record. 11. Record about sports opponents. (Rooney, 2003)

The Online Slang Dictionary
Book v 1. to leave quickly. ("When the police arrived, we booked.")
(Rader, 1997–2002)

Putting the colloquialism aside, these old definitions of *book* are no longer sufficient. The book is in the midst of a technological transformation, and the actual concept of book is changing as well.

The book is one of the main focal points and foundations of modern education. But as educators integrate new technologies into teaching, the book is undergoing a transformation to include what is known as the electronic book, or e-book. E-book formats go well beyond paper and binding and encompass a wide range of technologies, from CD storybooks, to audio books, to online books.

The goal of *The Digital Reader* is to explore the countless ways that the e-book may be applied to education, from a child reading an e-book for enjoyment, to one reading for research, to one using an e-book as a scaffold to improve reading ability. E-books have great potential to support learning and improve learning outcomes, offering new ways to integrate reading throughout the curriculum. The variety of book formats provides us, as teachers and students, with a range of tools for improving reading and learning.

E-books in the Information Age

In our information-oriented society, technology enriches our lives and surrounds us, from ATMs to cell phones. Our children are growing up in this technology-saturated world. According to the most recent U.S. Census results, there are now more homes in the U.S. that have computers than those that don't (U.S. Census Bureau, 2001). The educational system is part of this trend; most schools have some form of computer access for students.

As we move further into the Digital Age, the way we look at things is changing. Just compare a computer of 10 to 20 years ago with one of today. Similarly, our paradigm of the book needs to shift to encompass today's wide variety of book formats, both print and digital. And we as educators need to recognize the advantages, options, scaffolds, and supports that these digital forms present.

This technological revolution is being driven by three factors. The first is Moore's law of electronics, which indicates that computer systems have been doubling in capacity and speed every 18 months (with an associated decrease in costs). The second factor is that the amount of information in the world has been doubling every four years since before the turn of the last century. The third factor is the Internet, a system that allows for communication, sharing, and the transfer of information.

One huge advantage of e-books is their size—or lack of it. Many of today's students are overloaded by the amount of weight they carry in their backpacks. A study in Boston found that the average middle school student carried more than 20 pounds of books in a book bag (Petracco, 2001; see Figure 0.1). Considering the size and weight of a middle school student, this is simply too much. Doctors suggest that to avoid physical injury, one should never carry more than 10% of one's body weight (International Chiropractic Pediatric Association, 1998). Technology now allows a student to carry many books, references, and resources in a single hardware device, which may weigh as little as a pound. According to one e-book company, a gigabyte of memory could contain more than "200 illustrated college reference books, or 350 legal volumes, or about 2,500 600-page novels" in PDF format (Munyan, 1998). With the computer and technology infrastructure now available in a large number of schools, e-books can become a cost-effective and health-conscious alternative to bound texts.

Reading has been and continues to be a basic part of education, from the old three R's (reading, 'riting, and 'rithmatic) to today's No Child Left Behind. The printed word is central to our culture, and many teachers make reading the primary focus of education. Digital media, including electronic text, surpass the traditional forms in the ability to meet various student needs (Rose & Meyer, 2002). While reading may always be a constant in education, what may change is the way that we teach reading and the tools that we use. Electronic books are among the newest forms of "reading materials" that we can use in our teaching tool kit.

The other day I had an amazing experience while introducing an e-book to a third-grader. He was reading a print copy of *The Voyages of Dr. Dolittle*, the second volume in the Dr. Dolittle series, because his school didn't have the first. I went to a computer in the room, quickly downloaded and installed MS Reader, then accessed an online library and downloaded the first volume in the series, *The Story of Dr. Dolittle*. I showed the child how to start the program, select a book from the "library," advance pages, use the dictionary, and start the book reading aloud. By the time I stepped back, he had restarted the program, selected the Dr. Dolittle story, pressed the play (read aloud) button, and was entranced watching the screen as it highlighted the words while the program read them aloud. He was so focused on his reading that when he was asked to take part in something else, his reply was "Not yet, I want to get through chapter 3 first."

Today's students embrace technology in ways previous generations may have a hard time understanding. Reading words on a screen has always been part of their lives (Figure 0.2). Even less-experienced technology users can use electronic texts because many skills they've developed using print materials apply to using e-books. Most users quickly acquire any technical skills needed to use e-book software. Once e-books are introduced as a reading option, the next step is to help new users develop specific skills to meet their individual needs so that they recognize the potential advantages.

Figure 0.1. A popular comic highlights a very real problem for students.

Zits partnership. Reprinted with permission of King Features Syndicate.

As I watch the middle school children riding home on their bikes after school, I notice that some of them are talking on their cell phones. Children are naturally attracted to technology; as teachers, librarians, and media specialists, we should use that interest, and one way we can is with e-books. Electronic books are available, the tools are in the schools and in the students' homes, and it is time to start incorporating e-books into education.

As we look at the growth of technology integration into education and the need to make student resources more available, e-books provide an ideal solution. E-books may have the power to one day remove a large part of that 20-pound book bag that students are carrying. For many teachers and media specialists, you may now be looking at a resource that will allow schools to give books to students (books that they can *keep*) at no cost to the school or the child. These resources are easily updated and don't fill up shelf space.

Using E-books in Education

In many ways reading and instructional applications for using an e-book in the educational setting are no different than when using a printed book. A few days after I demonstrated e-books to an elementary teacher, she had set up e-book reading stations using the six computers in the back of her classroom. She showed her students how to use the e-books, and they were immediately employed for independent supplementary reading.

Using e-books in the classroom is an excellent application of technology. Whether accessed on a handheld, laptop, desktop, graphing calculator, cell phone, or even an MP3 player, electronic books are a reality of our lives, and we as parents, teachers, and school administrators should start maximizing their potential.

While there may come a day when digital books replace printed books in school, the current role of e-books is to supplement classroom reading material. What's more, e-books can be easily incorporated into classrooms and library collections using technology already in place, at no cost (Figure 0.3). To realize the advantages of e-books a school doesn't need to have a computer for every student, because electronic text can be used effectively with whole class, small group, individual, and center-based instruction.

Figure 0.2. A student reads an e-book on a desktop computer.

Features

E-books provide features that paper books cannot. With many e-books, users control the look and feel of the text within the e-book—they can write and save notes, highlight portions of text, and even draw, all within the e-book. E-books use computer memory for storage, so it is possible to put large numbers of books into small packages (Figure 0.3). Because of that computer interface, students have access to interactive dictionaries and Web hyperlinks; it is even possible to have the books read aloud. These tools and others provide scaffolding that can assist in student learning.

Figure 0.3. E-books can be stored and displayed on a variety of reading devices.

Accessibility

E-books can be used successfully no matter what the classroom configuration and no matter how many computers or reading devices are available. (This book does not go into depth concerning specialized e-book devices, as most schools would be unable to afford them.) Using e-books in the classroom requires that students have some access to computers or handheld devices, but it does not have to be 1-to-1 access. E-book files can be distributed to students through wireless connections, infrared beaming, e-mail, the Internet, or some form of storage medium, such as flash drives and CD-ROMs. The educator for a course can compile all the reading material from online sources such as newspapers, journals, and books along with documents and notes, and make it available to students electronically.

Availability

Numerous online libraries and bookstores distribute free or low-cost e-books that you can download to your e-book reading device for classroom use. These range from copyright-free texts that include much of classic literature, science, and philosophy to current bestsellers, reference books, and instruction manuals. The Internet Public Library, an educational initiative from the University of Michigan's School of Information, claims to have links to more than 40,000 e-books that can be read online or downloaded for free. To put it simply, a literature teacher can easily find hundreds of texts to give students at no cost. Teachers can use any sections of the books they need without worrying whether students will bring the correct texts to class. Or, instructors can add notes, organizers, comments, and questions before converting a text to an e-book format. Because the material is in an electronic format, students can copy and paste portions of text to use in reports, in notes, or for analysis.

Teaching Strategies

Teachers can also use e-books in conjunction with reading comprehension strategies to improve student abilities. Such strategies might include concept mapping, think-share-pair, KL (Know/Learned) diagrams, and one-sentence summaries. These strategies can be used either with individuals or cooperative groups.

Many e-books have the ability to track a student's progress, keeping a record of where they stopped reading. E-books also compile hyperlinked lists of annotations added while reading. Many digital books offer reading scaffolding tools, such as a read-aloud feature so students can hear text, and the ability to increase the text display size.

E-books are naturally suited to the language arts, but they are also available in a vast array of topics and can be excellent resources in various .

Meeting the Standards

A major driving force in our schools is standards. An effective standards-based classroom is a print-rich environment. Several standards support the use of e-books in schools. ISTE's National Educational Technology Standards for Students (NETS·S), for instance, specify that students use technology tools to enhance learning, increase productivity, and promote creativity, as well as to locate, evaluate, and collect information from a variety of sources (ISTE, 1998).

The NETS·S are compatible with selected Standards for the English Language Arts from the National Council of Teachers of English and the International Reading Association (NCTE & IRA, 1996), which state that:

1. Students read a wide range of print and nonprint texts to build an understanding of texts, of themselves, and of the cultures of the United States and the world; to acquire new information; to respond to the needs and demands of society and the workplace; and for personal fulfillment. Among these texts are fiction and nonfiction, classic and contemporary works.

The same NCTE/IRA standards also advocate that:

8. Students use a variety of technological and information resources (e.g., libraries, databases, computer networks, video) to gather and synthesize information and to create and communicate knowledge.

Improving Awareness of E-books

Unfortunately, while e-book availability has been growing, awareness by teachers and use by students have not grown. During a recent presentation on e-books to a state reading conference, composed of teachers and media specialists, most indicated that they had never heard of the concept and were unaware of the resources available.

In an initial study at a midsize university's college of education, 24 graduate students taking educational technology and 58 undergraduate students in reading education classes, mostly from elementary education programs, were assessed on their knowledge of and experience with e-books. Only 41% of the teachers and future teachers indicated that they knew what e-books were, and of those surveyed only 10% indicated that they'd had actual experience with them. In interest inventories on the concept of using e-books, the majority of students were only somewhat interested in e-books for themselves (53%), for their students (58%), or in educational situations (56%). When asked to describe a possible educational application of using e-books in schools, 45% of the respondents indicated that they didn't know of any applications (Cavanaugh, 2003).

A program is now taking place at the College of Education and Human Services at the University of North Florida in which undergraduate reading and English as a second language (ESL) courses educate students concerning e-books. In one professor's literature courses, all students are required to read an e-book of their choice and read another that would be appropriate for children that they expect to teach. After reading the e-books, students are asked to write a literature evaluation of the book, along with their personal experience in reading in this format.

Technology Integration

More than 300 years had passed between the time when Gutenberg made the first modern printed book and printed books were actually applied in school classrooms (Lockard, Abrams, & Many, 1997). That's quite a spell, and one hopes we wouldn't have to wait that long for the classroom implementation of e-book technology.

Caution, however, may be warranted. It is not appropriate to integrate a technology into the educational setting without evaluating its implications; we should not just use technology for technology's sake.

Neil Postman (1990) points out that every technology can give and take away. One purpose of this book is to help educators recognize the advantages that digital text can offer to education. And while electronic forms of text may or may not be the same as printed text, as Sven Birkerts (1994) questions, our students will have to work with electronic forms of text throughout their lives.

Home and School

Increase the reading relationship between school and home. Place selected e-books on a school Web site for students and parents to access from home.

We are experiencing the ongoing evolution of text. Information was once memorized and disseminated orally, then technology advanced and information was stored and disseminated in print on paper. Now we are moving into an age in which information is stored and disseminated through electronic methods. Our students will need to become as familiar with these digital tools as we once had to be with that large wooden card catalog at the front of the library.

Many people once thought that paperback or pocket books would never last or be accepted as real books. Now we have a new text medium that is integrating the possibilities of computer processing and resources with interactive capabilities. When will educators start to use these tools? How will students have interactions with these texts? What opportunities are unfolding to improve teaching with the advent of such tools? These are the questions and challenges facing educators.

Teachers who begin to explore these tools with their students will be in the forefront of the new text evolution and will be ensuring that students have the ability to select from as many tools for reading as possible. Electronic books are now available, and the tools for accessing them are in our schools and homes. The creativity of teachers will determine the long-term benefits that students realize from beginning their journey with this new communication format.

Objectives of This Book

The objectives of this book are to provide educators, administrators, librarians, parents, and anyone else with an interest in books and technology with:

- a functional understanding of e-books and their features
- the advantages of using e-book technology in presenting information

- the unique attributes of e-books that make them effective teaching tools and resources

- ways to apply e-books as personal productivity tools

- techniques for using e-books in classroom and professional settings

- e-book software and resources, such as online libraries

- suggestions for integrating e-book technology with other software applications to create educational resources

- information detailing the utility and flexibility of e-book technologies in meeting the needs of learners with various abilities, language backgrounds, and special needs

- sample e-book lessons, activities, and applications for a range of grade levels and content areas

Conclusion

In reading this book, I hope that you will learn to apply e-books in creating interactive educational activities and materials to support reading instruction, literacy, standards, and reading in the content areas. Numerous strategies have been developed for integrating e-books into reading instruction and remediation. E-books can help with a variety of reading problems. Educators can easily locate e-books to support reading in all content areas or use e-book software to create their own e-books on particular topics. No longer should schools take a "wait and see" attitude concerning book technology, as was done in the past. E-books offer tremendous possibilities to teachers, students, media specialists, librarians, and anyone with an interest in education.

Online Resources

Books

Drscavanaugh.org (e-book resources for education): www.drscavanaugh.org/ebooks/index.htm

LeapFrog (e-books for young children): www.leapfrog.com

Software

Adobe Reader: www.adobe.com

eReader: www.ereader.com/product/browse/software

Internet Explorer: www.microsoft.com/downloads

MS Reader: www.microsoft.com/reader

Netscape: http://channels.netscape.com/ns/browsers/default.jsp

Standards

English Language Arts Standards: www.ncte.org/about/over/standards/110846.htm

ISTE National Educational Technology Standards for Students: http://cnets.iste.org/students/s_stands.html

International Digital Publishing Forum: www.idpf.org
International trade and standards organization for the digital publishing industry.

References

Birkerts, S. (1994). *The Gutenberg elegies: The fate of reading in an electronic age.* Winchester, MA: Faber and Faber. Retrieved June 2005 from http://archives.obs-us.com/obs/english/books/nn/bdbirk.htm

Cavanaugh, T. (2003). E-books: An unknown reading option. In *Proceedings of Society for Information Technology and Teacher Education International Conference* (pp. 1387–1389). Norfolk, VA: Association for the Advancement of Computing in Education.

Houghton Mifflin. (2000). Book. In *The American Heritage dictionary of the English language* (4th ed.). Retrieved August 2005 from http://www.bartleby.com/61/2/B0390200.html

International Chiropractic Pediatric Association. (1998). *Back packs: Your child's spine at risk.* Retrieved October 2004 from http://www.4icpa.org/Articles/Nov98a.htm

International Society for Technology in Education (ISTE). (1998). *National educational technology standards for students.* Eugene, OR: Author. Also available online at http://cnets.iste.org/students/s_stands.html

Lockard, J., Abrams, P., & Many, W. (1997). *Microcomputers for twenty-first century educators* (4th ed.). New York: Longman.

Munyan, J. (1998). Proceedings from first international etext conference. Gaithersburd, MD.

The National Council of Teachers of English & the International Reading Association (NCTE & IRA). (1996). *Standards for the English language arts.* Urbana, IL: Author. Retrieved May 2005 from www.ncte.org/about/over/standards/110816.htm

Petracco, P. (2001, May/June). Weighing in on backpacks. *School Leader.* Retrieved November 2004 from http://www.njsba.org/members_only/publications/school_leader/May-June-2001/info_link.htm

Postman, N. (1990). *Informing ourselves to death.* Speech presented at a meeting of the German Informatics Society (Gesellschaft fuer Informatik) on October 11, 1990, in Stuttgart. Retrieved June 2005 from http://www.frostbytes.com/~jimf/informing.html

Rader, W. (1997–2002). Book. In *The online slang dictionary.* Retrieved August 2005 from http://www.ocf.berkeley.edu/~wrader/slang/

Rooney, K. (Ed.). (2003). Book. In *Encarta Pocket English Dictionary.* London: Bloomsbury.

Rose, D. H., & Meyer, A. (2002). *Teaching every student in the Digital Age.* Alexandria, VA: Association for Supervision and Curriculum Development (ASCD). Retrieved November 2004 from http://www.cast.org/teachingeverystudent/ideas/tes/

U.S. Census Bureau. (2001). *Home computers and Internet use in the United States: August 2000.* Retrieved April 2003 from http://www.census.gov/prod/2001pubs/p23-207.pdf

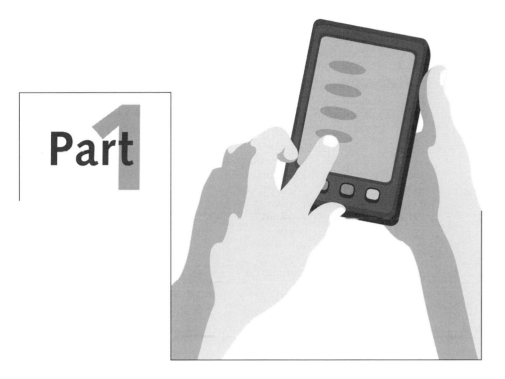

Part 1

E-book Technology

Choosing the Right Hardware and Software

First described in the science fiction of the 1940s, today e-books are real. You can find e-book readers on a variety of devices, from computers, to calculators, to MP3 players—even on cell phones.

Twenty-first century students have unprecedented access to technology. More than 90% have computer access (U.S. Census Bureau, 2001), and teens now spend more time online using the Internet than watching television (Patrick, 2004). Yet students are feeling a disconnect between their personal use of technology and their technology experiences in school. While a majority of online teens use the Internet for school-related research, they complain that their teachers aren't using the available technology and that Internet access at school is too slow (National Science Teachers Assoctation, 2002). E-books can help bridge the gap. The time is right for schools to start applying e-books, because the technology is there and the students are ready.

Chapter 1 offers a brief history of the e-book as well as an overview of devices, formats, features, and multimedia resources. Chapters 2 and 3 explore options for e-book hardware and software, respectively.

References

National Science Teachers Association (NSTA). (2002, October/November). Newsbits. *NSTA Reports.* Retrieved August 2005 from http://www.nsta.org/reports

Patrick, S. (2004, July). *E-learning and students today: Options for No Child Left Behind.* Speech presented at the No Child Left Behind Summit. Orlando, FL.

U.S. Census Bureau. (2001). *Home computers and Internet use in the United States: August 2000.* Retrieved April 2003 from http://www.census.gov/prod/2001pubs/p23-207.pdf

Chapter 1

The Electronic Book

The e-book is defined in various ways. It has been described as any material presenting text through a digital method, but also includes items such as books on tape, so it can also be considered any presentation of a book using modern technology. Another definition is that an e-book is a digital file, but not limited to just text, that is displayed on some form of computer or electronic device. According to Adobe Systems Incorporated (2002), e-books are digital reading materials that you view on a desktop or notebook computer, or on a dedicated portable device. E-books then are textual documents that have been converted and "published" in an electronic format that are displayed on e-book readers, devices, or computers using e-book software programs.

E-books, like many other forms of computer technology, have two basic components: hardware and software. The hardware for an e-book is any type of technology that displays the "book" on a screen or presents it audibly with a speaker. The software being run on the hardware makes it possible to view or listen to all of the "book" material: text, pictures, sound, and whatever else the author includes. Under this definition, even a DVD displaying closed-captioning qualifies as an e-book.

No Longer Science Fiction

Figure 1.1 provides a quick look at the developments in writing that have culminated in today's electronic books. The Sumerian cuneiform tablet is one of the oldest examples of human writing. The tablet gave way to the scroll, and the scroll to the codex around the time of Julius Caesar (50 B.C.). The next major change occurred in the mid-15th century with the refinement of the printing press. In 1452 Gutenberg created the movable type printing press, which used oil-based ink. Now, 500 years later, people are still making paper books, but we print on both sides.

Figure 1.1. An e-book timeline.

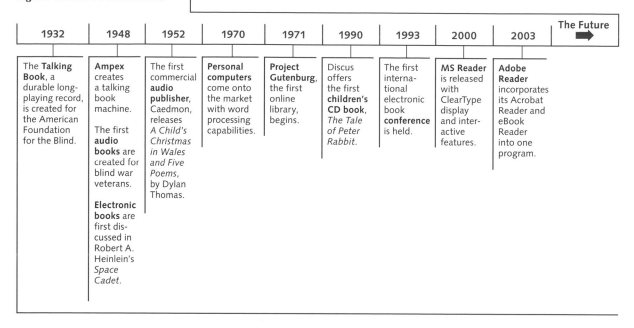

1932	1948	1952	1970	1971	1990	1993	2000	2003	The Future →
The **Talking Book**, a durable long-playing record, is created for the American Foundation for the Blind.	**Ampex** creates a talking book machine. The first **audio books** are created for blind war veterans. **Electronic books** are first discussed in Robert A. Heinlein's *Space Cadet*.	The first commercial **audio publisher**, Caedmon, releases *A Child's Christmas in Wales and Five Poems,* by Dylan Thomas.	**Personal computers** come onto the market with word processing capabilities.	**Project Gutenburg**, the first online library, begins.	Discus offers the first **children's CD book**, *The Tale of Peter Rabbit.*	The first international electronic book **conference** is held.	**MS Reader** is released with ClearType display and interactive features.	**Adobe Reader** incorporates its Acrobat Reader and eBook Reader into one program.	

The earliest mention of e-books appears to have occurred in a science fiction novel, Robert A. Heinlein's 1948 *Space Cadet* (Bryant, 2003; Figure 1.2). In the book, students use information "spools," which are displayed with projectors on their study desks. The handheld electronic book appears in Douglas Adams' 1979 *Hitchhiker's Guide to the Galaxy:* "It's a sort of electronic book. It tells you everything you need to know about anything. That's its job" (technovelgy, 2005). E-books continue as a sci-fi theme today, such as in Charles Sheffield and Jerry Pournelle's 1997 novel *Higher Education,* in which students use readers with optional voice output and variable video display. E-books have been a part of science fiction for years, and now they are also a part of 21st-century reality.

Figure 1.2. Book cover of Robert A. Heinlein's *Space Cadet*, the first book to mention electronic books.

© 1948, Charles Scribner's Sons, New York.

The first real e-books were created when people began using electronic resources such as word processors to create and store information. Floppy disk books were an experiment of the early 1980s, with publishers such as Book-on-Disc and Eastgate Systems. These floppy diskette books were limited by the small capabilities of the disks at the time along with the screen refresh rates and flicker issues that affected readability.

The floppy disk e-book was quickly replaced by the CD-ROM or "extended" form in the late 1980s (Crawford, 2000). The CD e-book quickly expanded into two main areas, the children's storybook and the digital encyclopedia. Both of these e-book forms were considered extended because they added to electronic texts through multimedia, hypermedia, and other interactive elements. Children's books included games, puzzles, tests, and audio enhancements. Publishers of encyclopedias were able to apply the increased storage ability of the CD-ROM to put an entire encyclopedia set onto a single compact disc, with hyperlinks between topics and articles, audio clips, and even some video. This form of e-book also introduced users to searching within the e-book (Eberhard, 1999). With the accessibility of so many titles on the Internet, CD-ROM e-books are usually limited to reference works and children's storybooks (Butler, 2000).

Electronic text was first shared on ARPAnet, an Internet prototype created in 1969 by the Department of Defense. In 1971 Michael Heart created Project Gutenberg (www.gutenberg. net), with the purpose of freely releasing public domain books through the Internet. Today, Project Gutenberg has more than 10,000 books available for free download, with mirror sites all over the world. In a 2002 interview, Heart stated that from just one Project Gutenberg site, more than a million e-books were downloaded in a single month (Vankin, 2002).

E-books achieved serious recognition in 1998, when the National Institute of Standards and Technology held the first international e-book conference. One of the big issues discussed was e-book format. Format is still in contention today, as evidenced by the number of formats in use (Munyan, 1998).

An Overview of Devices and Formats

The first thought that springs to mind when hearing about e-books is text displayed on a computer screen. But there are many different types of e-book, which can be accessed on a wide variety of devices (Table 1). Many of these make use of multimedia, combining text, audio, still images, video, and graphics.

> ### Copyright and Public Domain
>
> A **copyright** provides a set of exclusive rights to an intellectual property, such as literary works, movies and video, music, recordings, paintings, photographs, software, and industrial designs. The copyright protects the particular work created. Copyrights are granted by government agencies for a limited period of time.
>
> Once a work's copyright has expired, or if the creator failed to get or did not desire a copyright, the work becomes part of the **public domain**. Works in the public domain are ones in which no person or other legal entity can establish or maintain proprietary interests. All works created and published before 1923 are considered to be part of the public domain.

Figure 1.3. HP's Pocket PC handheld running MS Reader software for e-books.

Most people are familiar with audio books, which include books on tape, books on CD, and MP3 books. While many may have not considered it, most television programs and movies can be viewed using closed captioning, thereby creating a video e-book.

E-books are no longer limited to computers connected to the Internet. They can be stored and read on laptops, pocket computers that use operating systems such as Windows CE and Palm (Figure 1.3), and special e-book reading devices such as the LeapFrog LeapPad or the eBookwise-1150 (Figure 1.4).

One recent innovation has been e-books available for display on modern cell phones. The first cell phone e-book to receive a lot of attention was by an author in Japan named Yoshi who published a book titled *Deep Love* as a serial that was distributed as downloadable text files to be read on cell phones (Steuer, 2004). Within three years of its release the e-book's download site had accumulated more than 20 million hits. The book was then printed on paper and became a bestseller, and is now being made into a movie. While this technology seems to be focused in Japan right now, with the current proliferation of cell phones, it should only be a short while before it moves into the rest of the world.

These devices, explained more thoroughly in chapter 2, can all be used to read e-books:

- e-book reader (LeapPad, eBookwise-1150)

- handheld computer or PDA (Palm, Pocket PC, cell phone)

- personal computer (desktop, laptop, or tablet)

- audio device (tape, CD, or MP3 player)

- video device (television with VCR or DVD player)

Figure 1.4. The eBookwise-1150 handheld e-book reader.

Clearly, the huge variety of information devices allows people to access e-books anywhere. It has now become possible for a person to carry his or her own personal or professional library in a pocket for anytime access, storing the books on a computer chip not much larger than a postage stamp. Naturally, the device being used determines the software, or format, needed to read the e-book. For instance, DVD players have their own built-in software, a discussion of which is beyond the scope of this book. Rather, this book focuses on five common, freely available text formats, which I call the big five formats: plain text, HTML, Adobe Reader, eReader (formerly Palm Reader), and Microsoft Reader. All five can be read using a desktop, laptop, or tablet computer, or a handheld device. (See chapter 3 for a full exploration of software and formats.)

Table 1. E-book Devices and Media Types

	MEDIA TYPES		
	Text Format	**Audio**	**Video**
DEVICES	■ Handheld computer or PDA ■ Personal computer	■ Tape player ■ CD player ■ MP3 player ■ Book reader ■ Handheld computer or PDA ■ Personal computer	■ Television ■ DVD or VCR player ■ Handheld computer or PDA ■ Personal computer

An Overview of Features

Initially the text-format e-book was a single long Web page or text file that you could read by scrolling. If reading extended over more than one sitting, you had to remember where in the book you stopped in order to continue (Figure 1.5).

Figure 1.5. A Web e-book display. Note the scroll bar.

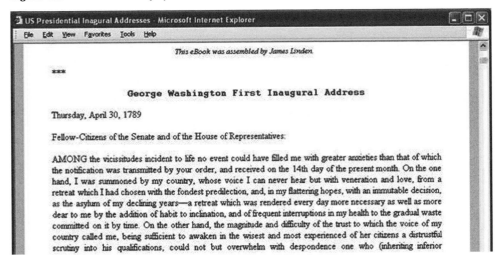

Today's text-format e-books, some of which are still published in plain text (TXT) or HTML, have gone far beyond that initial design to be much more user-friendly. Modern e-book applications are highly interactive. Through a combination of hardware and software, the books are displayed one page at a time, in a portrait orientation. Readers can adjust the text size, instantly find where they left off, highlight portions of the text, and search the entire book. Students can copy and paste text from e-books to use in reports, notes, or analyses. Interactive dictionaries are instantly available to look up unknown words. Students can also interact with the Internet by submitting forms or by starting browsers with hyperlinks to Web sites.

Figure 1.6. Annotation log of e-book interactions.

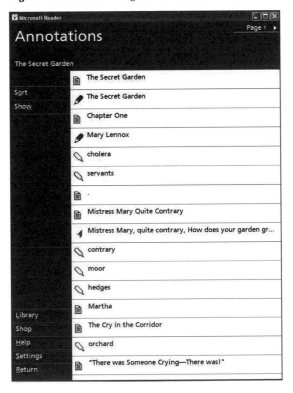

Many e-book readers support annotations, allowing students to take notes within the book itself. A single annotations file automatically saves all the notes, referencing the location of the notes within the book. Educators can distribute to students annotation files for assigned e-books, with content such as study questions. The annotations file can also include prepared accommodations for students with special needs, such as highlighting (see chapter 8).

Some e-book programs have more extensive features. They allow users to access dictionaries in multiple languages, highlight text in a variety of colors, write the equivalent of margin notes, "draw" in the book, and even create an annotation log to document e-book interactions, with hyperlinks to the location of the interaction (Figure 1.6). Some desktop or laptop e-book versions have a text-to-speech option that reads aloud and provides users additional modalities for receiving the information.

Multimedia E-books

While much of this book discusses text-format e-books, multimedia e-books should not be overlooked as great resources for the classroom. Here's a closer look at e-book formats that make use of multimedia.

Audio Books

Most people are familiar with audio books, as most schools, libraries, and bookstores have them on the shelf. The audio book may be considered an e-book, because it is made up of digital information that is presented with an electronic device. Audio books come in a variety of formats: books on records, books on cassette tapes, books on CD, and now even books in the MP3 format (Figure 1.7). You can download audio books from sources such as Audible (www.audible.com) and Audio Books for Free (www.audiobooksforfree.com), which have MP3 book files that you can listen to on a computer, hand-held, or MP3 player. Audio Books for Free is an online audio library that allows users to download abridged and unabridged books from more than 35 categories. Users at Audio Books for Free select the audio format of book they want, from multi-files at lower quality (8 Kb/sec) for free, to fewer files at higher quality (48 Kb/sec) for about $8 a "book."

Figure 1.7. Audio books.

Research findings indicate that hearing text read aloud improves reading ability. The use of audio books can assist students with reading comprehension. While some readers only need to see words, others benefit from also hearing them simultaneously. As Kylene Beers (1998) states in her online article *Listen While You Read,* "the use of audiobooks … is powerful since they act as a scaffold that allows students to read above their actual reading level. This is critical with older students who may still read at a beginner level. While these students must have time to practice reading at their level, they must also have the opportunity to experience the plot structures, themes, and vocabulary of more difficult books."

Electronic Storybooks on CD

Electronic storybooks on CD are quite popular with smaller children. The storybook CD is usually a self-running disc that does not need a special display program installed on the computer; instead, everything is on the CD (Figure 1.8). The first notable electronic book

Figure 1.8. Children's CD storybooks.

of this type was Discus's *The Tale of Peter Rabbit,* created in 1990 for the Macintosh. Since then, numerous electronic children's books have been made and sold. These e-books can be divided into two main types: electronic first and paper first. Electronic first are initially created and distributed in a digital version. Paper first are initially published as printed books and then transferred into an electronic format, usually with added material. These additions include enhancements and special features that improve the quality of the electronic version over the paper version.

For example, look at *Stellaluna,* a popular book that is quickly becoming a children's classic. This story itself is wonderful and beautifully illustrated, and has won numerous awards including the American Bookseller's Book of the Year Award, the Keyston to Reading Book Award, and the SCC Literature for Young People Award. The CD storybook version of *Stellaluna,* by Living Books, provides all the text and images from the book, but also includes much more, such as additional pictures, information about bat science, extra text material, quizzes, and extension activities. Most storybook CDs are also interactive: when a character or object is clicked on, he, she, or it may speak or perform some kind of action, such as sing or move. The CD version of the children's favorite *Chicka Chicka Boom Boom* not only plays as an audio book narrated by Ray Charles in a CD player, it can also display the story on a computer, provides games for children, and even allows children to sing along with the song and hear their own voice with the playback.

Television and Video with Closed Captioning

While we might not think of television programs or movies as e-books, with one simple menu choice, text can be displayed and a "book" appears. Research has indicated that turning on the captioning or subtitle feature can help students improve their reading while they are watching television (National Captioning Institute, 2004). Not only are most television programs captioned, most DVDs and videotapes have the ability to display subtitles, sometimes in a number of languages. As required from the Television Decoder Circuitry Act, all new televisions since 1993 with a screen size of more than 13 inches have closed-caption decoders built in. If none is built in, an external decoder can be attached. Even though closed-captioning technology is available on many TVs, many people have never gone through the television's menus and turned on the captioning (Figure 1.9).

As today's students have grown up with television as a constant companion, they are usually not reluctant to read from the TV, and it has been found that it has a motivational quality that is appealing to students, even ones that have been difficult to teach using traditional methods. If you want to do silent reading with closed captioning, just turn down the sound.

Figure 1.9. Closed captioning as an e-book is demonstrated in this screen capture from *Saving Springer*, an Emmy award-winning documentary from the National Oceanic and Atmospheric Administration.

Using closed captioning creates an additional option for reading practice. Many students I have encountered who are reluctant to read from printed material are quite happy to read from the television.

In one school where I taught we played videos over the network with the sound off, but the captioning on, and as you looked in the rooms you would see groups of students sitting around the television, reading the program, while others read from books and magazines.

Research has found that using the closed-captioning feature can help not only regular students but also special education students, second language learners, and even adults improve their reading ability (Feinberg, 2003).

Conclusion

Reading is the most ubiquitous educational activity. In the past, the importance of reading in the classroom meant having enough paper copies of a text to meet a class's needs. Today, the requirements of promoting literacy have shifted to include not only having the paper copies, but also having certain kinds of technologies to allow readers access to new forms of books. Fortunately these technologies are common in most schools. With these technologies we can drastically increase the number of text options available to our students, as well as provide alternative formats and supports for reading. E-books are available in many formats in a range of topics and can easily be adapted as educational materials, for reading or reference.

Online Resources

Booksellers

Audible (MP3 audio book seller): www.audible.com

LeapFrog (e-books for children): www.leapfrog.com

Captioning Service

National Captioning Institute: www.ncicap.org/index.asp
A nonprofit corporation researching captioning for people who are deaf or hard of hearing, as well as others who can benefit from the service.

Cell Phone Books

Bunko Yomihodai (Japanese only): www.kadokawa.co.jp

Shincho Keitai Bunko (Japanese only): www.shinchosha.co.jp

Space Town Books (Japanese only): www.spacetown.ne.jp

Libraries

Audio Books for Free (audio books): www.audiobooksforfree.com

Internet Public Library (multiple formats): www.ipl.org/div/reading/

Project Gutenberg (text-format e-books): www.gutenberg.net

History

National Institute of Standards and Technology: www.itl.nist.gov/div895/conferences.html

References

Adams, D. (1979). *The hitchhiker's guide to the galaxy.* Reprint, New York: Del Rey, 1995.

Adobe Systems Incorporated. (2002). *2000: Year of the e-book.* Retrieved July 2004 from http://www.adobe.com/epaper/features/newleaf/main.html

Beers, K. (1998). *Listen while you read.* Retrieved August 2005 from http://www.abcaudiobooks.com/Article4.aspx

Bryant, J. (2003). *Electronic books.* Retrieved January 2004 from http://www.luna.co.uk/~jbryant/pages/e-book.htm

Butler, T. P. (2000). Tale spinning: Children's books on CD-ROM. *The Horn Book Magazine, 73*(2), 219.

Cavanaugh, T. (2002, November/December). E-books and accommodations. *TEACHING Exceptional Children, 35*(2), 56–61. Available online at http://journals.sped.org/EC/Archive_Articles/VOL.35NO.2NOVDEC2002_TEC_Article%208.pdf

Crawford, W. (2000). Nine models, one name: Untangling the e-book muddle. *American Libraries, 32*(8), 56.

Eberhard, M. (1999, March 8). E-book economics (electronic books and the publishing industry). *Publishers Weekly, 246*(10), 22–23.

Feinberg, J. (2003). *Captioned television improves reading and literacy skills.* NEWSrelease from the National Captioning Institute. Retrieved October 2004 from http://www.ncicap.org/Educationrelease.asp

Heinlein, R. A. (1948). *Space Cadet.* Reprint, New York: Del Rey, 1992.

Munyan, J. (1998). Proceedings from first international etext conference. Gaithersburd, MD.

National Captioning Institute. (2004). *Using captioned television in reading and literacy instruction.* Washington, D.C.: Author.

Sheffield, C., & Pournelle, J. (1997). *Higher education.* New York: St. Martin's Press.

Steuer, E. (2004, June). Phone Fiction. *Wired Magazine.* Retrieved August 2005 from http://www.wired.com/wired/archive/12.06/play.html?pg=6

technovelgy. (2005). *Glossary of science fiction inventions.* Retrieved January 2005 from http://technovelgy.com/ct/ctnlistalpha.asp

Vankin, S. (2002). *The second Gutenberg.* United Press International. Retrieved August 2005 from http://promo.net/pg/upi_interview_05_02.html

Chapter 2

E-book Hardware

The hardware necessary to start using e-books can cost nothing, if you're making use of existing equipment. Any computer today can read e-books, and any DVD player can display a movie with closed captioning. Conversely, you could invest hundreds of dollars in specialized reading devices. (I discuss specialized reading devices only briefly, because most schools would not be able to afford them.) This chapter provides a look at the hardware typically available to most classrooms, and how it can be adapted to read e-books.

Hardware Devices for Text-Format E-books

E-books in a plain text format can be read using a standard desktop, laptop, or tablet computer. Handheld devices are another option, as most multifunction PDAs, such as a Palm, can easily read plain text.

No matter what tool is being used for display, e-books come in specific software formats, and users must have the appropriate associated software loaded on their device to read them (see chapter 3).

Computers

The most common text-format e-book display device is some form of computer: desktop, laptop, tablet, or handheld. This hardware is often the most appropriate for schools, as most schools already have standard computers and many also have handheld devices.

A teacher or librarian can build an e-book resource center out of a single computer in a classroom or library. This e-book station could then be used by individuals or groups for learning activities, or be used by an instructor to project a text onto a screen for the whole class. So at virtually no extra expense, a classroom, school, or school system could easily

Table 2. The Big Five Formats and Hardware Compatibility

	WEB (HTML/XML)	PLAIN TEXT (TXT)	ADOBE READER (PDF)	MICROSOFT READER (LIT)	eREADER (formerly Palm Reader) (PDB/PRC)
Windows Desktops (Windows 98 or greater)	Yes	Yes	Yes	Yes	Yes
Windows Laptops (Windows 98 or greater)	Yes	Yes	Yes	Yes	Yes
Windows Tablets (Windows 98 or greater)	Yes	Yes	Yes	Yes	Yes
Windows Handheld Devices (Windows CE 2.0 or greater)	Yes	Yes	Yes	Yes	Yes
Apple Desktops (Mac OS X or greater)	Yes	Yes	Yes	No	Yes
Apple Laptops (Mac OS X or greater)	Yes	Yes	Yes	No	Yes
Palm Handheld Devices (Palm OS 3.0 or greater)	Yes	Yes	Yes	No	Yes

add e-books to its technology repertoire without purchasing any extra hardware—just install the free software onto the existing hardware (Figure 2.1).

The Big Five Formats

While e-books are made in a range of styles, they will, for the most part, be available in five main formats, which I call the big five formats. Table 2 shows the compatibility of the big five e-book formats with various hardware devices. For more on these formats, see chapter 3.

Hardware Devices for Audio and Video E-Books

Audio

Audio books have already made their way to most school libraries. While the text of an audio book is not displayed, it is still delivered to the reader. The hardware required to listen to an audio book depends on its format. An audio book could require a record player for records or a cassette player for tapes. Books on compact disc can be played in a CD player or on a computer's CD drive. Audio books also come in MP3 format, which can be read on any computer using a program such as Windows Media Player or Apple iTunes, or on an MP3 player such as the Sony iPod.

Figure 2.1. This desktop computer is running several e-book programs

When using a computer to play an audio book for the class, instructors will probably prefer to use a set of exterior speakers over the computer's internal speaker. Headphones should be available for individual students to use when listening to an audio book or a text-to-speech book to avoid disruptive noise.

Video

Video hardware is also commonly found in most schools. For a video to become an e-book, the captions or subtitles will need to be displayed. Televisions of at least 13 diagonal inches manufactured after 1993 have closed captioning built in. The captioning can be turned on using the television's menu options. If the closed-caption decoder is not built in, external closed-caption decoders can be attached to any television for less than $100. If a DVD is the source, then either the DVD player will have captioning options accessible through the player menu or the DVD video itself will provide a menu option for displaying subtitles in English and often other languages. Most DVDs can also be viewed on a modern computer with a DVD drive and speakers.

Specialized Readers

For the most part, specialized handheld devices, such as the early Rocket e-book reader, did not succeed in the marketplace. Certainly, they were too expensive and fragile for school use. One of the biggest success stories concerning stand-alone e-book hardware in schools has been the LeapPad (Figure 2.2) and related devices from LeapFrog. The LeapPad is one of a few devices associated with a children's e-book format called Talking Books (Table 3). A hard copy book is set on the player and a cartridge placed in the reader. Students use a stylus to sound out, spell, and define words.

Table 3. Children's Talking Book Devices

DEVICE	NUMBER OF BOOKS	COST OF DEVICE	COST OF BOOK	INTERACTION	TEACHER'S MANUAL
LeapPad	170+	~$35	$7–15	Pen touch	Yes
PowerTouch	25+	~$35	$10–15	Finger touch	No
StoryReader	30+	~$25	~$9	Turn page	No
ActivePAD	16+	~$25	~$8	Pen touch	No

Prices based on Amazon.com and Froogle, April 2005.

Figure 2.2. A student uses a LeapFrog Talking Book.

The concept of reading devices is still a growing area; currently companies worldwide are developing new e-book devices, such as China's Q-Reader from Q-Net Technologies (Planet eBook, 2002) and Japan's LookPal from NEC (zmcnulty, 2004).

Conclusion

A variety of equipment can be used to access text-format, audio, and video e-books, and all have their unique qualities and characteristics. Teachers need to determine for themselves the hardware that will work best in their individual classrooms. This decision may be influenced by their budget and the equipment they have on hand. Keep in mind, however, that purchasing a few handheld devices on which to read e-books may save you money in the long run, as many e-books are free, while their paper counterparts are not.

With an understanding of the range of e-book reading devices, the next step in the e-book integration process is to look at the various software programs and e-book file types. The next chapter discusses e-book software, including the big five e-book formats.

Online Resources

Talking Books

ActivePAD/Publications International: www.myactiveminds.com/activepad/

LeapPad/LeapFrog: www.leapfrogschoolhouse.com, www.leapfrog.com

PowerTouch/Fisher-Price: www.fisher-price.com/us/powertouch/

StoryReader/Publications International: www.pilbooks.com/childrens/index.cfm/classname/Story%20Reader

References

Planet eBook. (2002). *Q-Net Technologies, Inc. introduces electronic reader.* Retrieved January 2004 from http://www.planetebook.com/mainpage.asp?Webpageid=387

zmcnulty. (2004). *Linux tablet-type device from NEC, "LookClub."* TechJapan discussion board. Retrieved March 2004 from http://www.techjapan.com/modules.php?op=modload&name=News&file=article&sid=201&mode=thread&order=0&thold=0

Chapter 3

E-book Software

When first introduced, e-books were a single long page in plain text or HTML format. A reader had to scroll line by line through text that wasn't always easy on the eyes.

Although some of today's e-books are still published in plain text or HTML, improvements in software enable them to be read with ease. For instance, text size and color can be adjusted. Other formats, such as Adobe Reader, Microsoft Reader, and eReader, provide features that improve on print books, such as instant access to dictionary definitions or annotated notes. Some software will even read the book aloud.

The Big Five E-book Formats

E-books come in a variety of formats. Five formats are the most common and freely available. These "big five" formats are plain text, HTML, Adobe Reader, Microsoft Reader, and eReader (formerly Palm Reader). All five can be read using a desktop, laptop, or tablet computer, or a handheld device. Table 4 shows a comparison of the capabilities of the big five formats.

Plain Text (TXT)

Plain text e-books can be read by any text reader or word processor. One freeware program, Tom's eTextReader, lets you read plain text files in a book-like manner. Window size, font style, and font size are selectable; page breaks are inserted automatically. This program makes is easy to read plain text e-books, such as those in the vast library of Project Gutenberg.

Figure 3.1. PDF e-books are read using the free Adobe Reader program.

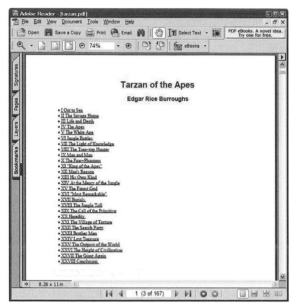

Adobe product screenshot reprinted with permission from Adobe Systems Incorporated.

Web (HTML/XML)

HTML e-books can be read with any Web browser. Using the capabilities built in to most Web browsers, such as Firefox and Internet Explorer, readers can adjust text styles, size, and colors. With HTML it is possible to search for terms within the book, and copy and paste selected text from the e-book to other programs.

Adobe Reader (PDF)

Adobe Portable Document Format (PDF) e-books can be read on Windows or Macintosh operating systems using a PDF reader, such as Adobe Reader. The PDF format allows for page navigation, multiple viewing options, adding bookmarks, and searching. Many consider the Adobe Portable Document Format a standard for electronic distribution worldwide, as PDF files are compact and can be easily shared, viewed, navigated, and printed (Figure 3.1).

Microsoft Reader (LIT)

Microsoft Reader e-books are compatible with Windows operating systems for desktop, laptop, and tablet computers as well as handheld devices. Microsoft Reader uses a technology called ClearType to make words on screen appear more like print. MS Reader's navigation system allows for multiple methods of page navigation and will remember where readers have stopped. MS Reader allows creation of annotation files and provides colored bookmarks and highlights, searching, and dictionary lookup features. MS Reader's current desktop, laptop, and tablet versions can also read text aloud. Users can change the highlighting colors, choose font sizes and styles, and add notes.

eReader (PDB)

E-books in the eReader format (PDB) can be read on handhelds, laptops, and desktops running the eReader program, which is available for virtually any platform. The eReader program allows users to select various fonts and font sizes, which controls the amount of text on the screen. The program also provides a rapid navigation system, bookmarks, and word search (Figure 3.2).

Figure 3.2. eReader is available for virtually any platform.

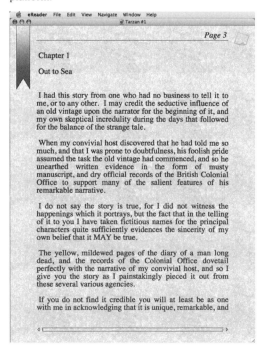

Table 4. Big Five E-book Format Comparison

	WEB (HTML/XML)	PLAIN TEXT (TXT)	ADOBE READER (PDF)	MICROSOFT READER (LIT)	eREADER *formerly Palm Reader* (PDB/PRC)
Portable Device	Yes	Yes	Yes	Can be used on laptops and Pocket PC devices	Can be used on Palm, Pocket PC, or laptop
Reader Cost	Free download	Free built-in	Free download	Free download	Free download (Pro version $9.95)
Printing	Yes	Yes	While the system has the ability, most publishers block this option	No	No
Number of Titles That Can Be Stored	Unlimited, depending on memory size	Unlimited, depending on memory size	Unlimited, depending on memory size	Unlimited, depending on memory size	Unlimited, depending on memory size
	1 copy of *Tarzan* takes up 479 KB	1 copy of *Tarzan* takes up 479 KB	1 copy of *Tarzan* takes up 331 KB	1 copy of *Tarzan* takes up 238 KB	1 copy of *Tarzan* takes up 219 KB
	A 1.44 floppy could hold 2 copies	A 1.44 floppy could hold 3 copies	A 1.44 floppy could hold 4 copies	A 1.44 floppy could hold 6 copies	A 1.44 floppy could hold 6 copies
	129 copies on a 64 MB card	133 copies on a 64 MB card	193 copies on a 64 MB card	268 copies on a 64 MB card	292 copies on a 64 MB card
Word Search	Yes	Yes	Yes	Yes	Yes
Bookmarking	No	No	Yes	Yes	Yes
Highlighting	No	No	Yes (if allowed)	Yes	Yes with Pro version
Note-Taking	No	No	Yes (if allowed)	Yes	Yes
Text-to-Speech	No	No	Yes	Yes	No

Continued

Table 4. Big Five E-book Format Comparison *(Continued)*

	WEB (HTML/XML)	TEXT (TXT)	ADOBE READER (PDF)	MICROSOFT READER (LIT)	EREADER *(formerly Palm Reader)* (PDB/PRC)
Synchronized Highlighting with Text Read-Aloud	No	No	No	Yes	No
Adjustable Text Size	Yes	Yes	No (only zoom)	Yes	Yes
Displays Pictures and Art	Yes	No	Yes	Yes	Yes
Allows Drawings in E-book	No	No	No	Yes	No
Interactive Dictionary	No	No	Yes (if online)	Yes	Yes with Pro version
Remembers Where Last Stopped	No	No	Yes	Yes	Yes
Display Navigation	Scroll	Scroll	Page at a time	Page at a time	Page at a time
Two-Page Display	No	No	Yes	No	Yes with Pro version

Other Formats to Consider

Formats other than the big five have their own mix of capabilities.

Print on Demand (POD)

One special e-book format is the POD e-book, or print on demand. A POD book is available digitally, but instead of being read on a screen, the book is printed paper. The Internet Archive Bookmobile (Internet Archive, 2004) uses POD technology. The bookmobile, which is associated with the Million Book Project (Carnegie Mellon University Libraries, 2004), drives across the country, stopping at schools, museums, and libraries. It allows visitors to choose from more than 20,000 public access titles. A title is downloaded, printed, and bound right in the bookmobile.

Figure 3.3. TumbleBooks are animated talking books.

TumbleBooks

Another special format is TumbleBooks (www.tumblebooks.com), designed for young children. TumbleBooks are animated talking books that play on most computer browsers that accept the Flash plug-in or by using the free TumblePad software (Figure 3.3). TumbleBooks, a division of Tumbleweed Press, offers a year-long subscription that provides online access to 50 TumbleBooks, quizzes, games, lesson plans, and worksheets (Tumbleweed Press, 2004). Those without online access can receive the library on CD-ROM.

Audio and Video Software

Audio and video e-books make use of the same multimedia software that music and videos do. For audio books, the computers found in most schools will already have the software installed to play audio CDs or MP3 files. Common programs include Windows Media Player, RealPlayer, QuickTime Player, Apple iTunes, and Musicmatch Jukebox (Figure 3.4). Books on MP3 can also be played with an MP3 player, such as the iPod.

Besides the typical combination of a television and VCR or DVD player, most videos can be read or viewed on a modern computer. The computer needs to have a DVD drive, speakers, and a DVD player software program. Well-known programs include PowerDVD or WinDVD Platinum for the PC and Apple DVD Player for the Mac.

Figure 3.4. An audio e-book being played on a computer using Windows Media Player.

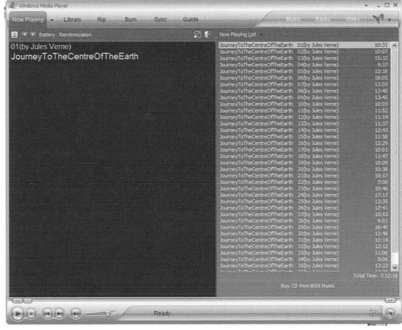

Choosing the Right Format for Your Classroom

What format will work best in the classroom? There is no easy way to answer that question. The decision will largely depend on the hardware and software resources already in place in the classroom, as well as the type of e-book activities that a teacher plans to incorporate in the curriculum. The following three scenarios show factors that teachers in different settings should consider when choosing an e-book format for the classroom.

Ms. Afonso teaches early elementary, Grade 3. Her classroom has three Macintosh computers running OS X that are connected to the school network and to the Internet through a class filter. She has decided to use her Web browser to access e-books. Most of the children's books she wants to use can be read with a browser running standard plug-ins such as Flash and Adobe. Also, most of her students already have experience with Internet browsers. Each day during reading time, her students take turns accessing children's story sites, such as Reading is Fundamental's Reading Planet and StoryPlace. They may also use the computer's browser and headphones to listen to and read along with stories presented in Flash format.

Mr. Beck is a special education teacher in a middle school. While most of his students are with him all day, he does have a few students who are in inclusion programs and spend part of their day with other teachers. His classroom has six Windows 2000 computers, all connected to the school network, but access to the Internet is restricted to approved sites. To encourage reading, Mr. Beck needs an e-book program for a wide variety of books. He also wants to provide reading accommodations such as text-to-speech and large-print options. Mr. Beck decides to have the school network specialist install MS Reader software on his classroom computers. Mr. Beck works with students at his desk to find e-books that interest them and then transfers the files to the classroom computers. For example, one student likes westerns, so Mr. Beck has placed a number of Zane Gray novels, available for free from Blackmask Online, on the computers. Students may read from the e-books whenever they have spare time. Others use the e-books as a reading strategy to meet their IEP plans, or use the e-books while working in groups during reading instruction. Students can adjust the size of the text to a comfortable setting. Many read along with the computer as it uses the text-to-speech feature to read the book aloud. When students start the MS Reader software, the e-books available are listed in the software's library.

Ms. Coontz teaches language arts in a high school. Her classroom has two computers, one new Apple Macintosh desktop for students and a Windows XP laptop for herself, both with network and Internet access. She also has access to a Windows-based computer lab on a sign-up basis. Because she needed a cross-platform program, she chose the eReader software. This allows her to install the software on both classroom computers and have the media specialist install the software throughout the lab. Using eReader or the Web browser already in the machines, her students have access to a large number of literature classics, including the collected works of Shakespeare, downloaded from the Electronic Text Center at the University of Virginia Library. Students use the classroom computer as a research and

[**Lesson**Idea]

Research Center

Set up a computer in a classroom that has access to online research e-books such as atlases, thesauruses, dictionaries, and encyclopedias. Encourage students to use them whenever they need to look something up.

reference station. Ms. Coontz uses her computer with a video projector to display important passages of text for discussion. The class also uses the computer lab on a weekly basis for literature circle activities. Ms. Coontz has also created a class Web page with links to the sites where course e-books can be downloaded, so her students can download them at home.

Conclusion

To decide which e-book format is the most appropriate for any specific classroom situation, educators will need to analyze the learning environment. Things to consider include the technology that is available, the skill level of the students, and any special interactions desired, such as text-to-speech or note-taking. Experiment with each of the big five formats to determine which best fits a given class.

Online Resources

Booksellers and Libraries

Blackmask Online: www.blackmask.com
This site offers more than 10,000 texts in a variety of formats, including LIT, HTML.

Electronic Text Center at the University of Virginia Library: http://etext.lib.virginia.edu/
Thousands of XML, HTML, MS Reader, and eReader texts are listed.

Internet Archive Bookmobile: www.archive.org/texts/bookmobile.php
This is a print on demand mobile digital library

Million Book Project: www.ulib.org
This is an online e-book library, with thousands of titles.

Project Gutenberg: www.gutenberg.net
Groundbreaking site with thousands of e-books.

RIF Reading Planet: www.rif.org/readingplanet/content/read_aloud_stories.mspx
RIF provides a collection of read-aloud books that changes monthly, in Flash format.

StoryPlace: www.storyplace.org
More than 20 stories for elementary children are offered, along with suggested readings and print out activities.

TumbleBooks.com: www.tumblebooks.com
Online books for children are offered.

Software

Adobe Reader: www.adobe.com

eReader: www.ereader.com/product/browse/software

Internet Explorer (Web browser that can display Web-based e-books): www.microsoft.com/downloads

Firefox (Web browser that can display Web-based e-books): www.firefox.com

Microsoft Reader: www.microsoft.com/reader

Netscape (Web browser that can display Web-based e-books): http://channels.netscape.com/ns/browsers/default.jsp

Tom's eTextReader (e-book reader program for reading plain text e-books; can also edit): http://pws.prserv.net/Fellner/Software/eTR.htm

References

Carnegie Mellon University Libraries. (2004). *Libraries projects: Million Book Project.* Retrieved December 2004 from http://www.library.cmu.edu/Libraries/LibProj.html

Internet Archive. (2004). *Internet Archive Bookmobile.* Retrieved December 2004 from http://www.archive.org/texts/bookmobile.php

Tumbleweed Press. (2004). *TumbleBooks.* Retrieved January 2005 from http://www.tumblebooks.com

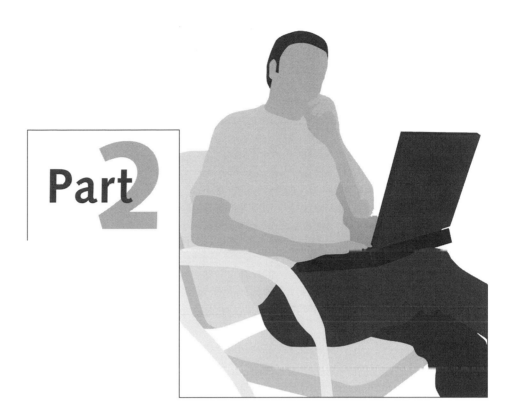

Part 2

Educational Applications

Using E-books in the Classroom

The concept of literacy is changing. The Internet and other forms of information and communication technology such as word processors, Web editors, presentation software, and e-mail are redefining the nature of literacy. To become fully literate in the Digital Age, a student must become proficient in technology.

Educators should integrate information technology into their curriculum to prepare students for the future. The International Reading Association (IRA) believes that much can be done to support students in developing the new literacies. IRA (2002) states that students have the right to:

- teachers who are skilled at using new literacies for teaching and learning;

- a curriculum that integrates these new literacies;

- instruction that develops these literacies for effective use;

- assessment practices in literacy that include electronic reading and writing;

- opportunities to learn safe and responsible use of information and communication technologies; and

- equal access to information and communication technology.

While the text of an e-book is displayed on an electronic device, the use and applications of e-books in the classroom are no different from paper-based material. Strategies for reading, the structure of the text, and the purposes for reading are still the same, but the e-book can bring to the classroom additional reading supports and can expand the number of books available to students. The time and effort required to learn this new technology will be rewarded with benefits the technology can bring.

E-books can be used in a variety of classroom technology configurations and in all subject areas. Chapter 4 explores strategies for classrooms with a variety of technology resources, from a single computer to one for every student. Chapter 4 also provides valuable resources for each content area.

E-books can provide additional tools when teaching reading strategies, such as digital high-lighting in different colors for different concepts (chapter 5). Other strategies an educator can apply include digital forms of text questioning, concept mapping, think-share-pair, KL (Know/Learned) diagrams, one-sentence summary, and features analysis, using either the individual or cooperative format.

E-books can provide more options for reading materials, and present text in different ways. For example, a number of children's picture books are available as e-books (chapter 6). Some of these are in video form, providing each student a person to read to them. E-books also have built-in supports that can help reluctant readers (chapter 7) and students with special needs (chapter 8).

Regardless of the student age or subject taught, educators can integrate e-books as tools with reading comprehension strategies to improve student abilities.

Reference

International Reading Association. (2002). *Integrating literacy and technology in the curriculum: A position statement.* Newark, DE: Author.

Chapter 4

E-books Across the Curriculum

Introducing e-books to the classroom isn't difficult. As a teacher, you will need to consider how best to manage the use of e-books in your classroom, taking into account the number of computers your students can access.

In addition to classroom management, this chapter takes a look at that staple of the classroom, the textbook, many of which are now available in electronic form. Because trade books supplement textbooks in most classrooms, this chapter also explores how trade e-books can be used in various content areas, with real-world examples.

Classroom Management with E-books

Students need hardware to access e-books at school. They need desktop, laptop, tablet, or handheld computers, or they need specialized e-book readers. The common technology configurations in schools are:

- the one-computer classroom
- classrooms with two or more computers in a center
- one-to-one computing either in the regular classroom or at a dedicated location

E-books may be used successfully in each of these settings.

The amount of time an individual student can spend with the technology varies greatly depending on the classroom's technology configuration. With greater access to technology, more options unfold for using e-books in the classroom (Table 5).

Using e-books provides a great solution for teachers seeking to use technology already on hand, as well as provides numerous reading options to students. According to the International Reading Association (2000, p. 3), "school libraries and classrooms must have an adequate amount of reading material for each child in order to create a fair balance between children who receive access to books outside of school and those who do not." At the same time, students have reported that schools and teachers don't make good use of the Web as a classroom tool (National Science Teachers Association, 2002). Accessing the large number of e-books on the Internet provides a low-cost solution to beefing up a school's library as well as an effective way to use classroom computers.

Managing Student Access

For technology integration strategies to flow smoothly, teachers should establish procedures for managing both the technology resources and student access to those technologies. For example, teachers might create some form of technology "passport" that tracks student use, with stickers to indicate turns.

Table 5. E-book Applications in Various Classroom Settings

CLASS DESIGN	ACTIVITIES
One Computer	Audio book listening station for individuals or whole class.
	Presentation station for digital big books.
	Download station for students to download e-book files onto personal storage media.
	E-book print station for printing either partial or complete documents.
	Reader's workshop station for having a computer read aloud (using synchronized highlighting with text-to-speech).
	Reading station for use by individuals; similar to a classroom book shelf for open reading time.
	Research station for use by individuals or small groups.
	Resource station for use by individuals as a reading support tool. For example, using enlarged text or text-to-speech capabilities (with headphones).
Center with Two or More Computers	*All the one-computer activities listed above as well as the following:*
	Literature circle stations for group work.
	Reader's theater (interpreting and orally presenting written text; see the description later in this chapter).
Whole Class or One-to-One Computing	*All the one-computer and two-or-more-computers activities listed above as well as the following:*
	Whole class reading stations where all students can follow along as a single book is read.
	Sustained silent reading stations where each student selects a book for individual reading.

Another idea is to hang a string horizontally near the technologies with student names written on clothespins, which could be moved to show a student's place in "line." With younger students a teacher may wish to use a point system, in which students gain points for completing work on time, being prepared for class, or working well together. Students could redeem points for technology access or checkout.

For groups, a teacher may wish to schedule set times for a series of center activities. When a group is at the reading center, members of that group would have the option of choosing a technology-delivered reading material.

Providing Specific Instruction

Students may need instruction on effective ways to read and use electronic texts. With some minor instruction on electronic text reading strategies, students can make much more effective use of the readings. Remind students to use the find feature to search for text strings, to set up interactive dictionaries, and to use digital note-taking strategies to make the reading experience more productive.

Remember, any of these e-book strategies can transfer to print materials. The tools and materials change, but the learning strategies remain the same. With a full-featured e-book reader such as Microsoft Reader, teachers have a program that can be used to boost a student's reading comprehension in numerous ways. See chapter 5 for more on using e-book features in reading instruction.

Depending on their abilities and experiences, students may also need instruction on the computer itself, including using removable media, network file storage, e-book software, Internet sites, and audio controls. To help students, teachers can place near the computer a reference sheet or poster showing the common steps for using e-books on the computer. As is true of any classroom technology, more experienced peers can assist less experienced students.

Hyperlinks to Class Readings

Instead of students having their own copies of e-books, you can direct them to specific Web pages for readings. Providing printed lists of lengthy Web addresses has its drawbacks—it's often difficult to effectively type in URLs. A better approach is to create HTML pages with hyperlinks to the readings.

If you don't have the ability or resources to create your own HTML pages, you can accomplish the same thing using a tool such as TrackStar (http://trackstar.4teachers.org; see Figure 4.1). TrackStar allows an instructor to create an annotated Web pathway to take students to a series of online readings. Working with its tools, students can take electronic notes, organize information, and gather citations on the readings.

Using another tool, it's even possible to store online reading materials for offline access. Using offline browsing tools, students can select sites they're assigned to read. The computer will download and hold the sites for later. One such tool, AvantGo (www.avantgo.com), works with handheld devices, downloading the Web site to the handheld computer the next time the device is synchronized with the docking station.

Figure 4.1. The Trackstar Web site allows teachers to create an annotated Web pathway to take students to a series of online readings.

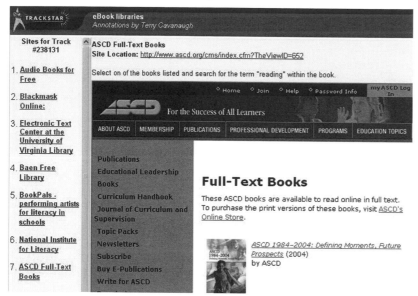

Carrying a Library with You

The most common complaint from students about using e-books is that they must read in a specific location, in a less-than-comfortable chair positioned in front of a computer screen. With today's laptop and handheld devices, this doesn't have to be the case (Figure 4.2). Using a memory storage card, I carry more than 50 books on my handheld device, some for education and some for entertainment, which I can read anywhere.

Electronic Textbooks

The textbook is a basic component of most courses. While instructors may want students to use and learn from a variety of textbooks, the cost of textbooks in recent years has risen into the double digits. University and other reports indicate that from 1983 to 1993, campus textbook costs increased more than 90%, and since 1998 textbook costs have risen an additional 41% (Schumer, 2003; Toner, 1998; Montclair State University, 2000; Christendom College, 2003).

With today's technology, it's possible to bypass the printed resource and use electronic text as part of the course reading materials. The main reasons for using electronic materials as text-

Figure 4.2. A student reads her course textbook on a handheld device that holds more than 50 e-book files.

books include accessibility, cost, currency of the material, and access to materials no longer in print.

Many quality electronic texts are available for student use through online libraries and other resource sites. Electronic versions of textbook material offer access to writings that may still be in the developmental phase or were recently updated. Companies that offer electronic versions of textbooks include McGraw-Hill (http://mhln.com), Pearson Prentice Hall (www.phschool.com), and Holt, Rinehart, and Winston (www.hrw.com/it/index.htm).

McGraw-Hill has developed a collection of texts in electronic format for the K–12 and higher education markets, and has more than 35 textbooks online for second grade through high school in literature, science, math, social studies, and languages. The McGraw-Hill Higher Education unit working with MetaText has converted more than 30 textbooks in economics, communication, English, biology, and geoscience (http://metatext.com; see Figure 4.3).

Holt, Rinehart, and Winston offers an added feature for some digital textbooks, a resource called Live Ink. Live Ink provides reading support through visual cues of the content to assist struggling readers, special-needs students, and English-language learners.

For some courses the electronic textbook may be the ideal format, such as courses taught through Internet-based distance learning. This use of an e-book as the text makes the book immediately available to the students. Yet the electronic textbook isn't limited to special classroom situations, and can be used as one of the standard texts in most situations. Another reason for changing from print to electronic versions of some textbooks is that the books may no longer be available in paper print.

There are various formats and approaches to using e-books as class textbooks. Electronic textbook sections can be downloaded from the Internet as they are needed. They can be provided to students on a storage medium, such as a CD. Or, they can be stored in document or HTML format (on a school district network or Web pages) for students to visit for reading.

No matter the format selected, there are advantages and disadvantages associated with electronic textbooks compared with traditional print textbooks (Table 6). Instructors must analyze the situation to decide whether the use of electronic textbooks will provide students with better access to reading materials.

Table 6. Advantages and Disadvantages of Using Electronic Textbooks

ADVANTAGES OF ELECTRONIC TEXTBOOKS	DISADVANTAGES OF ELECTRONIC TEXTBOOKS
■ Cost (depending on book) ■ Scaffolds and supports built in ■ Hyperlinks to other resources ■ Text-to-speech features ■ Direct linking to sections of books ■ Weight of book ■ Text searching ■ Annotation logs	■ Book desired unavailable ■ Format differences with printed versions ■ Internet access needed ■ Computer access needed ■ Lack of hard copy to reference sections in class

Figure 4.3. Kenneth S. Saladin's *Anatomy and Physiology* is one textbook for older students offered by McGraw-Hill Higher Education.

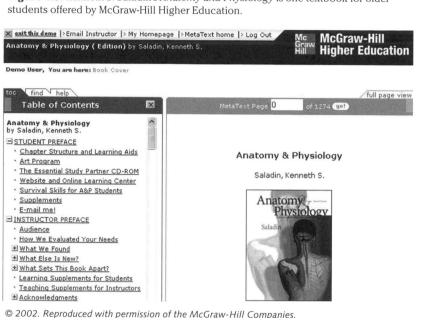

© 2002. Reproduced with permission of the McGraw-Hill Companies.

E-books for the Content Areas

Electronic books provide reading materials for both literary and technical reading, and most modern standardized reading assessments use both. Educators can find for their students e-books from many sources or entire electronic libraries devoted to specific subjects. In this section, I'll describe some of the books and libraries that can be used within content areas.

Most of these resources are trade books rather than textbooks. According to McGowan and Guzzetti (1991), using trade books exposes students to a wide range of resources presented in a variety of formats and writing styles. These diverse resources help students understand and develop concepts related to the topic, as well as discover connections to their own life experiences.

The content areas presented here are language arts and reading, science, mathematics, foreign language, social studies, and other subjects. An introduction to each content area is followed by "In the Classroom," a scenario that demonstrates how e-books can be used in teaching the subject. A resource list of specific online sites follows.

Language Arts and Reading

A literature teacher can download hundreds of texts to give to students at no cost. For example, the complete works of William Shakespeare are available from the University of Virginia Library at http://etext.lib.virginia.edu/shakespeare/works/ and from Project Gutenberg (www.gutenberg.org).

In an evaluation I performed, 27% of the suggested K–12 reading material for language arts in the state of Florida could be obtained at no cost to students, teachers, or schools with Internet access. The highest percentage available for a grade level was 70% of the required reading for 11th grade, or 16 out of 23 books (Cavanaugh, 2003). Visit www.drscavanaugh.

Figure 4.4. The OKAPI! site provides a readability analysis on text pasted in its CBA probe tool.

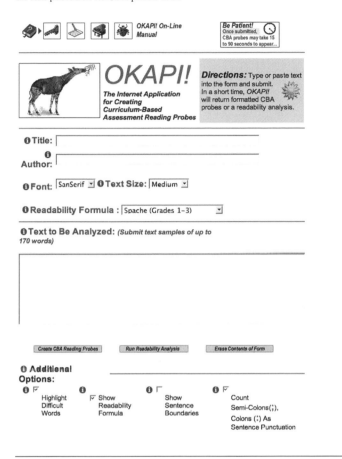

org/ebooks/ to see the reading lists and associated free e-books.

E-books can also be used in the creation of assessments, such as a curriculum-based assessment (CBA) reading probe. A useful resource for creating CBA probes is the OKAPI! site at www.interventioncentral.org/htmdocs/tools/okapi/okapi.shtml (Figure 4.4). Using public domain digital libraries, a teacher can paste up to 170 words into the OKAPI! online tool. The site then performs a readability analysis of the material, using either the Spache (Grades 1–3) or Dale-Chall (Grades 4 and up) formula, and creates an instructor tool and student reading sheet for a CBA probe. With OKAPI!, an English teacher can quickly create a range of CBA probes to assess student reading levels and abilities.

In the Classroom (Fifth Grade)

Ms. Bliss, a fifth-grade teacher, was concerned about her students' reading ability. She wished to assess her students more often, but also wanted to use reading materials that interested her students. She decided to use the OKAPI! CBA reading probe tool. First, she polled her students to discover reading topics that appealed to them. Using that list, she visited a number of e-book libraries and online newspapers and magazines. She found books and articles matched to the students' interests at the appropriate grade level. Next, she copied selections from the texts into the OKAPI! site and used the site to create the reading assessments, which she printed out and placed in each student's folder.

Ms. Bliss made at least three assessment instruments for each student. She had each student read aloud individually as she used the reading probe to assess the student. She also provided students with links to the Web sites from which the reading material in the probe originated, in case they were interested in reading more—and many were. From this experience Ms. Bliss felt the students had a more positive outlook on reading assessment. Instead of being a dry test, the assessments introduced the students to reading material that interested them.

In the Classroom (10th Grade)

Mr. Nichols is a 10th-grade language arts teacher in a suburban school. After polling his students to find out how many had access to the Internet outside of school, Mr. Nichols discovered almost all of his students had their own computers at home. The others said they commonly used the computers available at the school, the public library, and the community center to help them with their homework. After collecting this information, Mr. Nichols decided to make use of electronic books available on the Internet. This stretched his book budget and saved him time because he didn't have to order the books, check them out, or keep track of the returns.

The e-books also allowed him to integrate technology to develop student competencies in the language arts. His students were studying American literature, and he decided to have them take part in a literature circle activity based on books that focused on locations in the U.S. This activity met the state language arts standards (Florida Department of Education, 2002), including:

Diagram a Sentence

Using an e-book reader program, such as MS Reader, have students highlight words in a sentence in colors to represent the parts of speech. For example verbs could be in red, nouns in green, and pronouns in blue.

1. Demonstrate use of effective reading strategies to construct meaning from a range of representative American literature and related topics.

2. Demonstrate knowledge of various elements of American literature (e.g., theme, plot, setting, point of view, symbolism, character development).

Mr. Nichols selected five American classics: Thoreau's *Walden*, Hawthorne's *The House of Seven Gables*, Lewis's *The Octopus*, Wharton's *The Age of Innocence*, and James's *A Turn of the Screw*. Each of these books is available as a free e-book. The lesson plans included making reading available outside of class through a Web page with multiple links to each book in different e-book reader formats.

To determine the rosters for the literature circles, Mr. Nichols visited each of the book's Web sites and copied the first chapter into his word processor. Next, he wrote a short description of the book and added it to the first chapter. He then printed out a copy of each of the first chapters along with its story description. Mr. Nichols used the school copy machine to duplicate his printouts to create five sets of first chapters and descriptions. In class the students reviewed the descriptions and selected, in order of preference, which literature circle they wished to be in. Mr. Nichols used the selections to put the students in groups of five, and gave them the first chapter copies.

Mr. Nichols also assigned each group member a role in the literature circle. The students read the first chapter in class, and then had their first role activity and group discussion. The students were told to come prepared to discuss the next chapter in two days.

When the students participated in their literature circles in class, they had access to the five classroom computers as research tools. The students used the computers to search within their e-books for specific quotes or facts, and to look up associated references on the Internet.

Language Arts and Reading E-books

The e-books available for literature studies are tremendously varied. Rather than attempt to present a comprehensive list of literature titles, an 11th-grade reading list is provided below to give an idea of the scope of choices for a single grade. All of these titles are free.

1984, George Orwell (multiple formats): www.blackmask.com

Adam Bede, George Eliot (multiple formats): www.blackmask.com

Frankenstein, Mary Shelley (multiple formats): www.blackmask.com

Ivanhoe, Walter Scott (multiple formats): www.blackmask.com

Jane Eyre, Charlotte Bronte (multiple formats): www.blackmask.com

The Light That Failed, Rudyard Kipling (multiple formats): www.blackmask.com

Lord Jim, Joseph Conrad (multiple formats): www.blackmask.com

The Mayor of Casterbridge, Thomas Hardy (multiple formats): www.blackmask.com

The Moonstone, Wilkie Collins (multiple formats): www.blackmask.com

Of Human Bondage, Somerset Maugham (multiple formats): www.blackmask.com

Plunkitt of Tammany Hall, William L. Riordon (TXT): www.gutenberg.org/etext/2810

The Return of the Native, Thomas Hardy (multiple formats): www.blackmask.com

Silas Marner, George Eliot (multiple formats): www.blackmask.com

Sons and Lovers, D. H. Lawrence (multiple formats): www.blackmask.com

The Tempest, William Shakespeare (multiple formats): http://etext.lib.virginia.edu/shakespeare/works/

Tom Jones, Henry Fielding (multiple formats): www.blackmask.com

Tristram Shandy, Laurence J. Sterne (multiple formats): www.blackmask.com

Vanity Fair, Willam Thackeray (multiple formats): www.blackmask.com

Victory, Joseph Conrad (multiple formats): www.blackmask.com

The Way of All Flesh, Samuel Butler (multiple formats): www.blackmask.com

Science

E-books are excellent resources for scientific inquiry. The United States Geological Survey (USGS; www.usgs.gov) has an online library of books about geology including topics such as volcanoes, radon, and even the Moon. While learning about biology, students can read the books written by Charles Darwin, such as *The Voyage of the Beagle* or *The Origin of Species*. You can even find e-books that contain table and chart information, such as tables of formulae and the periodic table of the elements (Figure 4.5).

In the Classroom

Ms. Goodrich is a middle school science teacher in a rural school district. She was starting her unit on the Moon and wanted to engage her students in a variety of activities targeting different learning styles (kinesthetic, visual, and technological). Her goals were that her students would become familiar with the phases of the Moon and be able to explain the reasons for the lunar phases with regard to the orientation of the Sun, Moon, and Earth. She had only three computers in her classroom, one for herself and two for student use. She wished to expose the students to some of the literature that includes the Moon, and decided to use Jules Verne's *From the Earth to the Moon* (1865). Because of the limits of computer access for her students, she used her computer connected to a video projector to display selected portions of the book, and she had the students act out or discuss the descriptions. The following passage is from chapter 4:

> The motion of rotation is that which produces day and night on the surface of the moon; save that there is only one day and one night in the lunar month, each lasting three hundred and fifty-four and one-third hours. But, happily for her, the face turned toward the terrestrial globe is illuminated by it with an intensity equal to that of fourteen moons. As to the other face, always invisible to us, it has of necessity three hundred and fifty-four hours of absolute night, tempered only by that "pale glimmer which falls upon it from the stars."
>
> Some well-intentioned, but rather obstinate persons, could not at first comprehend how, if the moon displays invariably the same face to the earth during her revolution, she can describe one turn round herself. To such they answered, "Go into your dining-room, and walk round the table in such a way as to always keep your face turned toward the center; by the time you will have achieved one complete round you will have completed one turn around yourself, since your eye will have traversed successively every point of the room. Well, then, the room is the heavens, the table is the earth, and the moon is yourself." And they would go away delighted.

Figure 4.5. E-books can be useful in science, such as this e-book on the periodic table of the elements.

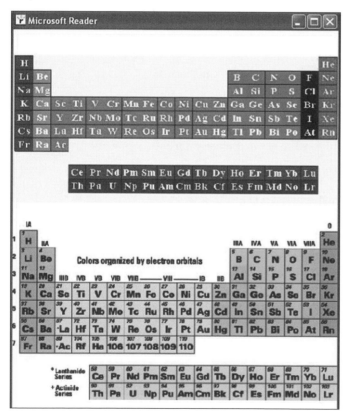

After she read the passage aloud to the students, each group performed the rotation from the passage and discussed how the same side of the Moon always faces the Earth.

Her students were also asked to observe the Moon over a period of several weeks, noting that the Moon rises and sets at different times each night, and the progression through lunar phases. To assist the students in understanding Moon phases, Ms. Goodrich had them read Jocelyn Bergen's *Satellite Story*. Ms. Goodrich downloaded the e-book from a Web site and printed out a master copy on 11" x 17" paper. She then used the school copier to duplicate the book so that every student had a copy. The students cut and folded the single sheet to make an eight-page booklet about the Moon phases. She had her students read from the booklet, and then used the booklet as a tool to help the students understand Moon phases. Her students at home used the booklet during their lunar observations to identify the lunar phase.

Science E-books

Bird Neighbors, Neltje Blanchan (LIT): www.abacci.com/books/

The Chemical History of a Candle, Michael Faraday (HTML): www.fordham.edu/halsall/mod/1860Faraday-candle.html

Faraday as a Discoverer, John Tyndall (HTML): http://selfknowledge.com/437au.htm

From the Earth to the Moon, Jules Verne (multiple formats): www.blackmask.com

History of Science, V1–V4, Henry Smith Williams (multiple formats): www.blackmask.com

The Life of the Caterpillar, J. Henri Fabre (HTML): www.ibiblio.org/eldritch/jhf/cater.html

The Origin of Species by Means of Natural Selection; or the Preservation of Favoured Races in the Struggle for Life and *The Voyage of the Beagle,* Charles Darwin (multiple formats): www.blackmask.com

Periodic Table of Comic Books (use of elements; HTML): www.uky.edu/Projects/Chemcomics/

Satellite Story, Jocelyn Bergen (PDF): www.zephyrine.com/satellite/index.html

The Strange Life of Nikola Tesla, Nikola Tesla (multiple formats): www.blackmask.com

The Student's Elements of Geology, Sir Charles Lyell (TXT): www.gutenberg.org/etext/3772

The Yosemite, John Muir (HTML): www.sierraclub.org/john_muir_exhibit/writings/the_yosemite/

Your Genes, Your Choices: Exploring the Issues Raised by Genetic Research, Catherine Baker (HTML): http://ehrweb.aaas.org/ehr/books/

Mathematics

E-books on mathematics include Newton's *Principa Mathematica,* books on fuzzy logic, children's counting picture books, and even *Flatland: A Romance of Many Dimensions* (Figure 4.6).

In the Classroom

Ms. Lee teaches early elementary students in an urban school. Her classroom has five laptop computers connected to the network, one for the teacher and four for students. Additional classroom computers are available for checkout or can be shared among teachers. Ms. Lee is starting her class on an interdisciplinary unit on economics. She will teach her students about cultures along with consumer economics and

Figure 4.6. *Flatland: A Romance of Many Dimensions,* by E. A. Abbot, is a mathematics classic.

fundamental economic principles, such as money recognition and basic math. Her students will take part in activities about earning money, spending money, and saving money. From these activities students should understand goods and services, needs and wants, and the difference between producers and consumers. As part of the activities, the students will participate in a classroom "market," where students will sell or barter goods.

To introduce the lesson, Ms. Lee will read the books *It Takes a Village*, by Jane Cowen-Fletcher, and *Grandma and Me at the Flea (Los Meros Meros Remateros)*, by Juan Felipe Herrera and Anita DeLucio-Brock. Both books are available in print from her school library and in digital form from the International Children's Digital Library (ICDL) at www.icdlbooks.org.

Both stories are about children participating in a community market—one during market day in a small village in Benin, the other in a flea market in Southern California. First, the students will discuss their shopping experiences. Next, Ms. Lee will connect to the ICDL and project the stories onto the screen in the front of the class as she reads to the students. While Ms. Lee reads the stories, the students will be tasked to identify the goods available in the markets, which she will write on the board.

When both stories have been read, the class will discuss consumer goods from the stories and from their own experiences. Following this, the students will rotate through different activity centers. One center will be set up as the classroom market. Another center will be set up as a reading area, with two of the classroom computers displaying the ICDL books accompanied by paper copies of the books from the school library.

Math E-books

Calculus Formulas, David Collet (LIT): www.e-librarie.ro/carte.php?id=517

Counting to Tar Beach, Faith Ringgold (PDF): www.icdlbooks.org

Euclid's Elements, Oliver Byrne's edition (HTML): http://sunsite.ubc.ca/DigitalMathArchive/Euclid/byrne.html

Flatland: A Romance of Many Dimensions, Edwin A. Abbot (HTML): www.geom.uiuc.edu/~banchoff/Flatland/

Fuzzy Systems: A Tutorial, James F. Brulé (HTML): www.austinlinks.com/Fuzzy/tutorial.html

Grandma and Me at the Flea/Los Meros Meros Remateros, Juan Felipe Herrera and Anita DeLucio-Brock (HTML): www.icdlbooks.org

Helping Children Learn Mathematics, Center for Education (HTML): www.nap.edu/books/0309084318/html/

Introduction to Probability, Charles M. Grimstead and J. Laurie Snell (PDF): www.dartmouth.edu/~chance/teaching_aids/books_articles/probability_book/book-5-17-03.pdf

It Takes a Village, Jane Cowen-Fletcher (HTML): www.icdlbooks.org

Mathematics and Art, Marc Frantz (PDF): www.math.iupui.edu/m290/Math-Art.pdf

Principia Mathematica, Isaac Newton (LIT): www.e-librarie.ro/carte.php?id=683

Teaching Mathematical Thinking Through Origami, Daniel Meyer, Aviva Meyer, and Jeanine Meyer (HTML): http://rachel.ns.purchase.edu/~Jeanine/origami/

Foreign Language

E-books solve what has often been a problem for foreign language teachers, finding interesting resources in the target language, because most local bookstores don't stock many foreign language books. Teachers of foreign languages, including English as a second language instructors, can use online libraries from around the world to provide reading materials that students can use for practice within their target language. See chapter 6 for information on picture book applications for foreign or second language students.

Microsoft gives away six translation dictionaries for MS Reader that you can use with foreign language e-books (Figure 4.7). Users can place these dictionaries into the My Library folder and use them to look up words defined in English or English words defined in Spanish, French, or German.

The International Children's Digital Library (www.icdlbooks.org) has children's books in more than 27 languages. Other libraries, such as the Libros Tauro (www.librostauro.com.ar/), Biblioteca Virtual do Estudante de Língua Portuguesa (www.bibvirt.futuro.usp.br/index.php), and Athena (http://un2sg4.unige.ch/athena/; see Figure 4.8), have thousands of e-books in their collections.

Several e-book programs work with foreign language text-to-speech readers, allowing students to have e-books read to them in other languages. The IBM Home Page Reader program (www-3.ibm.com/able/solution_offerings/hpr.html) can read Web-based e-books in English, French, and Spanish. The MS Reader program works with multiple text-to-speech packages, including English, French, and German (www.microsoft.com/reader/developers/downloads/tts.asp). Using one of these systems, a student can download an e-book written in a foreign language and have the e-book program read the text aloud, using the other language's enunciation structure.

In the Classroom

Mr. Ponti teaches Spanish in a middle/high school in a language lab where each student has a computer. The lab's language learning software allows students to verbally interact with the computer. In

Figure 4.7. A foreign language e-book is being used along with a translation dictionary in MS Reader.

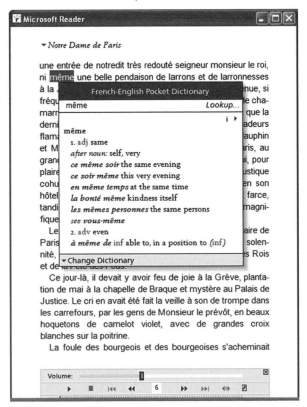

Figure 4.8. French and Swiss texts are available at the online library at Athena.

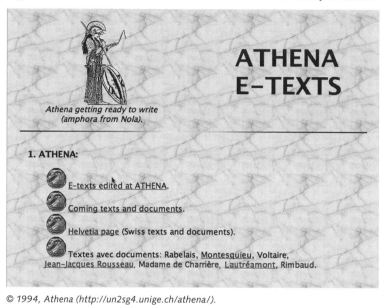

© 1994, Athena (http://un2sg4.unige.ch/athena/).

addition to students having proficiency in conversational Spanish, course objectives include demonstrating comprehension of written Spanish and using Spanish beyond the school setting. To achieve these objectives, Mr. Ponti has students read works of literature and newspapers written in Spanish. The computers in his room have the MS Reader program installed, and Mr. Ponti has downloaded a number of e-books to the computer's library folder. He also has created a set of links that his students can use to visit Spanish newspaper sites.

As part of his daily routine, at the beginning of each class, Mr. Ponti goes online to uComics.com, a comic strip site that provides Spanish versions of popular comics. He uses his video projector to display a comic strip in Spanish. The students translate the comic as their warm-up activity for each day's class.

Foreign Language E-books

Chinese

> *The Black Sun*, Li Si Si (HTML): www.icdlbooks.org

French

> *Une Grande Petite Fille/A Big Little Girl*, Ana Maria Machado and Dominique Osuch (HTML): www.icdlbooks.org

> *Notre-Dame of Paris/The Hunchback of Notre Dame*, Victor Hugo (multiple formats): www.blackmask.com

Spanish

> *Bisa Bia, Bisa Bel*, Ana Maria Machado (HTML): www.icdlbooks.org

> *The Bold Parrot and Other Jungle Stories*, Horacio Quiroga (HTML): www.icdlbooks.org

> *Don Quijote*, Miguel de Cervantes (multiple formats): www.blackmask.com

> *Magic Dogs of the Volcanoes/Los perros mágicos de los volcanes,* Manlio Argueta and Elly Simmons (HTML): www.icdlbooks.org

> uComics.com: www.ucomics.com/comics/
> More than 15 comic strips translated to Spanish, with archives of the current month.

Swahili

> *City Eyes*, Ruth Wairimu Karani and KHAM (HTML): www.icdlbooks.org

German

> *Die Verwandlung/The Transformation,* Franz Kafka (multiple formats):
> www.blackmask.com

> *Warum der kleine Delphin Purzelbäume schlägt/Why the Little Dolphin Tumbles Head
> over Heels,* Ana Maria Machado and Ulises Wensell (HTML): www.icdlbooks.org

Software

> IBM Home Page Reader (Web browser that can read aloud in multiple languages):
> www-3.ibm.com/able/solution_offerings/hpr.html

Social Studies

Geography teachers have a great resource in the CIA's World Factbook (www.cia.gov/cia/publications/factbook/), which provides information and maps on every country (Figure 4.9). Another great resource is the International Children's Digital Library (www.icdlbooks.org) for picture books on people and cultures around the world. For history lessons, a teacher might integrate works by Native American or African American writers from the University of Virginia eText Library (http://etext.lib.virginia.edu/ebooks/subjects/subjects-natam.html) or apply the Making of America collection (http://cdl.library.cornell.edu/moa/) from the Cornell University Library, which is a digital library of primary sources including 22 magazines from the 1830s to 1900s.

In the Classroom

Ms. Nana teaches junior high social studies in a suburban school. Her classroom has two computers: a laptop for her use and a desktop for student use. Two of the required benchmarks for the course are "use maps, globes, charts, graphs, and other tools of geography to gather and interpret data and to draw conclusions about physical and human patterns," and "locate and describe the physical and cultural features of political regions" (Florida Department of Education, 2005). Since she has only one computer for student access, that computer is a dedicated research station.

In addition to the regular encyclopedia software, she has downloaded and installed the CIA's World Factbook. Because the

Figure 4.9. The Central Intelligence Agency's World Factbook is updated annually.

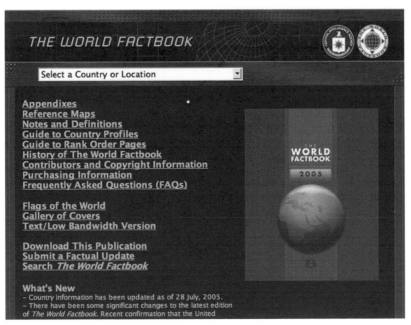

World Factbook is updated each year, the information is current. During class, whenever a new country is mentioned, a student is chosen to summarize the information about the country for the entire class, using the World Factback as a resource. That student then uses the word processor to make a page that has the name and short description of the country, an image of the flag, and a small map of the country. This page is printed and posted on the class bulletin board.

Social Studies E-books

Amistad Argument, John Quincy Adams (multiple formats): www.blackmask.com

The Autobiography of Benjamin Franklin, Benjamin Franklin (multiple formats): http://religionanddemocracy.lib.virginia.edu/library/historical.html

CIA World Factbook (online and downloadable HTML book about every country in the world): www.cia.gov/cia/publications/factbook/

Declaration of Independence (HTML): www.archives.gov/national_archives_experience/charters/declaration.html

Diary of Juan Bautista de Anza and other original journals from the Spanish expedition to found San Francisco (HTML): http://anza.uoregon.edu/

Impressions of an Indian Childhood, Zitkala-Sa (multiple formats): http://etext.lib.virginia.edu/ebooks/subjects/subjects-natam.html

Indian Why Stories, Frank B. Linderman (multiple formats): http://etext.lib.virginia.edu/ebooks/subjects/subjects-natam.html

The Rights of Man, Thomas Paine (multiple formats): www.blackmask.com

State of the Union Addresses, Abraham Lincoln (multiple formats): www.blackmask.com

Up from Slavery: An Autobiography, Booker T. Washington (multiple formats): http://etext.lib.virginia.edu/ebooks/subjects/subjects-afam.html

U.S. Presidential Inagural Addresses, various (multiple formats): www.blackmask.com

Woman's Half-Century of Evolution, Susan B. Anthony (multiple formats): http://etext.lib.virginia.edu/ebooks/subjects/subjects-women.html

Other Subjects

E-books are plentiful for non-core subject areas. In physical education, e-books are available on health, human anatomy, and sports rules. Art instruction can integrate e-books concerning museum collections, individual artists, and photography. E-books can even be used to put on plays or to implement reader's theater.

Reader's Theater

Reader's theater is a strategy for improving student skills and interest in reading through interpreting and orally presenting written text (Owocki, 2001). It can also be used to allow students to create dramatic narrations of passages from novels, short stories, and other works (Booth, 2001). This strategy has the students reading directly from scripts, without having to memorize lines. Students should be encouraged to use volume, pitch, intonation, facial expressions, and gestures appropriate to the character (Beers, 2003). Props, make-up, costumes, and stage settings are optional.

One difference between a reader's theater presentation and a play is that a narrator is required for reader's theater and is essential for describing the action, setting, transitions, and background. Collections of plays and scripts that can be used for drama productions are available from a number of online libraries, such as the drama section of Blackmask Online (www.blackmask.com/cgi-bin/newlinks/page.cgi?g=Drama%2Findex.html&d=1). On his Web site (www.aaronshep.com/rt/RTE.html), Aaron Shepard offers more than 35 reader's theater scripts adapted from stories that he and others have written, for students ages 8–15.

In the Classroom

Ms. Summers is a new teacher at a private high school and has been assigned to teach the drama class. Her students have put on a few plays in the past but said they were bored with the same titles that everyone else was doing, and that they wished to do a comedy. Ms. Summers was also looking for a play that she could use to help meet one of the course standards, that students should identify theatrical forms of various genres, cultures, and playwrights, as well as identify the influence of society and politics on dramatic themes. With these goals in mind, Ms. Summers looked for a comedy play that had social elements. At the Blackmask Online drama library, she found the play *Hobson's Choice* (Figure 4.10).

[**LessonIdea**]

Class Play

Download a play from an online library such as Reader's Theater Editions (www.aaronshep.com/rt/RTE.html) or Blackmask Online (www.blackmask.com). Open the play with a word processor and then print out student sheets to read from. The play's vocabulary can be edited in the word processor to make it easier for students.

Figure 4.10. The e-play *Hobson's Choice*, by Harold Brighouse, is now in the public domain.

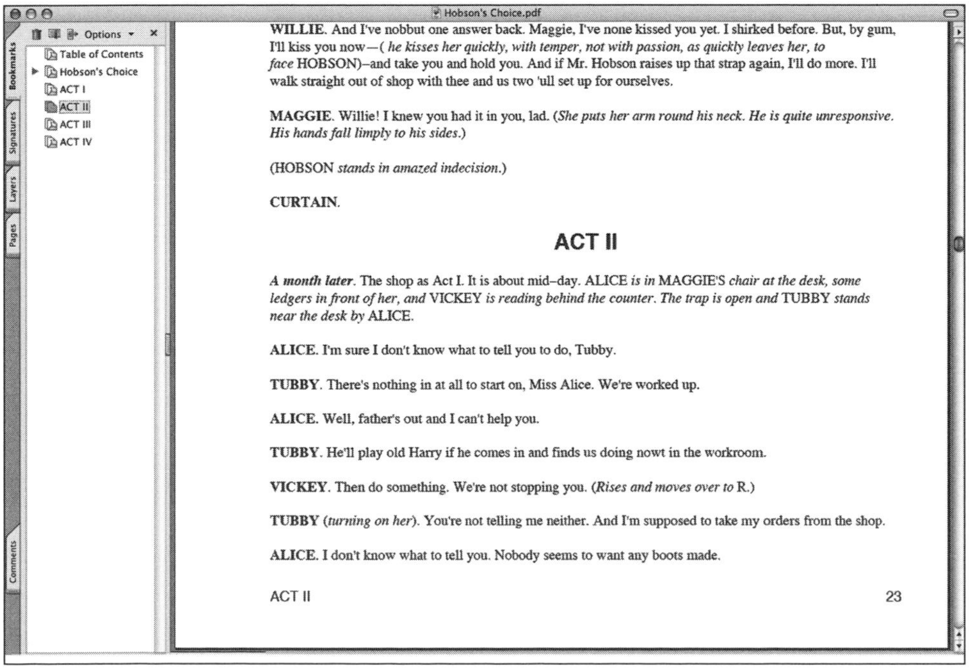

Hobson's Choice is the story of Henry Hobson, the alcoholic and tyrannical owner of a shoemaker's shop, his three daughters, and William Mossop, a shoemaker. This light comedy recognizes human failures and the human spirit, but also develops on the shifting balance of power between the generations, sexes, and classes that occurred at the turn of the last century. The online script has the speaking parts, along with the stage and set directions.

The play is now in the public domain, which means that the school would not be required to pay production royalties, saving the school hundreds of dollars per production. Ms. Summers downloaded the play to her computer and printed out individual scripts for the student actors and stage hands.

Other Subject E-books

Ayn Rand and Business, Ayn Rand (LIT): www.mslit.com/default.asp?mjr=FRE&mnr=FRE000075&sort=mp

The Downloadable Impressionists, ScalaVision (LIT): www.childrenselibrary.com/singletitle.php?productID=11688

Encyclopedia of Modern Music (PDB): www.memoware.com/?global_op=download_file&file_id=16708

First Aid Reference (multiple formats): www.absoluteword.com/aid1st/dl.htm

Hobson's Choice, Harold Brighouse (multiple formats): www.blackmask.com/cgi-bin/newlinks/page.cgi?g=Drama%2Findex.html&d=1

Optical Art, Paul Camacho (LIT): www.blackbirdfreepress.com/art.htm

Photoshop 6 for the Web (HTML): www.dzfx.com/workshops/list/2/Photoshop_6-For_The_Web/

Reader's Theater Editions (free scripts adapted from stories by Aaron Shepard and others; HTML): www.aaronshep.com/rt/RTE.html

Recipes Tried and True, Marion, Ohio, First Presbyterian Church Ladies' Aid Society (TXT): www.gutenberg.org/etext/1084

Rules of Golf (HTML): www.usga.org/playing/rules/rules.html

Washington, D.C.: The Rough Guide, Jules Brown (LIT): www.mslit.com/details.asp?bookid=1858289351

Conclusion

Once the decision is made to incorporate e-books into the curriculum, a tremendous range of options becomes available. Many educators are already making use of Web pages to direct students to readings, such as those in the resource lists presented in this chapter. Another important step is to integrate electronic textbooks, either as a complete text or compiled from many sources. The tools for electronic readings are available; the students have the technology and the access; now the educators just need to create the reading list.

Online Resources

Libraries

Athena Texts Francais (French and Swiss): http://un2sg4.unige.ch/athena/

Biblioteca Virtual do Estudante de Língua Portuguesa (Portuguese language library featuring Brazilian authors): www.bibvirt.futuro.usp.br/index.html?principal.html&2

Blackmask Online (free library): www.blackmask.com

childrenselibrary (e-book service for teachers and schools): www.childrenselibrary.com

International Children's Digital Library (free library): www.icdlbooks.org

Internet Public Library (free library and book links): www.ipl.org

Libros Tauro (Spanish library): www.librostauro.com.ar/

Project Gutenberg (free e-books): www.gutenberg.net

United States Geological Survey (digital Earth science nonfiction library): http://pubs.usgs.gov/products/books/glp.html

University of Virginia Library (a collection of SGML and XML-encoded text and images): http://etext.lib.virginia.edu/

Services

Drs. Cavanaugh (e-book resources and links): www.drscavanaugh.org/ebooks

Making of America (digital magazine collection): http://cdl.library.cornell.edu/moa/

OKAPI!: www.interventioncentral.org/htmdocs/tools/okapi/okapi.shtml
OKAPI! performs Dale-Chall or Spache readability analyses or creates curriculum-based assessment probes.

Software

IBM Home Page Reader (Web browser that can read aloud in multiple languages): www-3.ibm.com/able/solution_offerings/hpr.html

Microsoft Text-To-Speech Packages (English, French, and German): www.microsoft.com/reader/developers/downloads/tts.asp

Textbook Sellers

Amazon.com (used and new): www.amazon.com

MetaText (digital textbooks bundled with interactive tools): http://metatext.com

Textbook Publishers

Holt, Rinehart, and Winston (Grades 6–12 digital textbooks): www.hrw.com/it/index.htm

McGraw-Hill Learning Network (K–12 online textbooks): http://mhln.com

Pearson Prentice Hall (a leading publisher for secondary education): www.phschool.com

References

Beers, K. (2003). *When kids can't read: What teachers can do: A guide for teachers 6–12.* Portsmouth, NH: Heinemann.

Booth, D. (2001). *Reading and writing in the middle years.* Portland, ME: Stenhouse Publishers.

Cavanaugh, T. (2003). *E-books: An unknown reading option.* Paper presented at the Society for Information Technology and Teacher Education (SITE) conference, Albuquerque, NM.

Christendom College. (2003). *Fees and financial aid.* Retrieved October 2003 from http://www. christendom.edu/admissions/feesfaid.shtml#books

Florida Department of Education. (2002). *Course description—grades 9–12, adult.* Retrieved August 2005 from http://www.firn.edu/doe/curriculum/crscode/basic612/912/912/la912/1005310.PDF

Florida Department of Education. (2005). *Course descriptions for basic education.* Retrieved August 2005 from http://www.firn.edu/doe/curriculum/crscode/basic612/sost68.htm

International Reading Association (IRA). (2000). *Providing books and other print materials for classroom and school libraries: A position statement.* Newark, DE: Author.

McGowan, T., & Guzzetti, B. (1991). Promoting social studies understanding through literature-based instruction. *The Social Studies, 82,* 16–21.

Montclair State University. (2000, April 10). Faculty urged to meet textbook adoption deadline. *Insight.* Retrieved October 2003 from http://www.montclair.edu/pages/Publications/Insight/ BackIssues/2000/Insight041000/story2.html

National Science Teachers Association (NSTA). (2002, October/November). Newsbits. *NSTA Reports.* Retrieved August 2005 from http://www.nsta.org/reports

Owocki, G. (2001). *Make way for literacy! Teaching the way young children learn.* Portsmouth, NH: Heinemann; Washington, DC: NAEYC.

Schumer, C. (2003, October 10). *Schumer reveals local college textbook prices are skyrocketing—and proposes new $1,000 tax deduction to help cover cost* (Press Release, Senator Charles E. Schumer, New York). Retrieved October 2003 from http://www.senate.gov/%7Eschumer/SchumerWebsite/ pressroom/press_releases/PR02101.html

Toner, E. (1998, February 3). Tax break, state priorities debated. *The State News.* Retrieved August 2005 from http://www.statenews.com/editionsspring98/020398/p1_commit.html

Verne, J. (1865). *From the Earth to the Moon.* Reprint, electronic text.

Chapter 5

E-book Reading Strategies

Reading strategies, literature circles, reading workshops, and guided reading groups are all part of a balanced literacy program. Traditionally, literacy has focused on the ability to read words on paper, including books, newspapers, and job applications. Congress, with the 1991 National Literacy Act, defined literacy as "an individual's ability to read, write, and speak in English, and compute and solve problems at levels of proficiency necessary to function on the job and in society, to achieve one's goals, and develop one's knowledge and potential" (National Institute for Literacy, 1991). This new definition goes beyond paper to include reading from computer screens and personal devices, and includes media, technology, information, and other critical literacies (Semali, 2001).

According to Kress (2003), today's world places less emphasis on writing and more emphasis on other representational modes, which have evolved with new media forms such as computers, CD-ROMs, e-mail, chat rooms, cell phones, and handheld computers. Kress (2003, pp. 120–121) explains that "literacy and communication curricula rethought in this fashion offer an education in which creativity in different domains and at different levels of representation is well understood, in which both creativity and difference are seen as normal and as productive."

Along these lines, James Gee (1989) purports that in a modern society being technologically literate can lead to an individual's success. Chris Bigum and Colin Lankshear (1998) believe that today's teachers must re-perceive literacy and how technologies are used, so that they become more resonant with the situation that exists outside of schools. Teachers need to be able to provide rich literacy experiences that integrate technology for students of the Digital Age.

To support this goal, I adapted reading strategies to work with electronic formats and developed the e-Book Reading Strategies (eBRS) program, which is the focus of this chapter. The eBRS program is designed to assist students with the metacognitive process as they learn how to learn. It provides active strategies to help them organize, understand, and absorb material.

The eBRS Program

While for the most part any reading strategy can be used with an e-book, the digital nature of the e-book provides added support to certain reading strategies. The eBRS program takes interactive techniques that have been used with print material and applies the technology enhancements available with e-books, providing strategies for discussion, reading, writing, vocabulary, and assessment.

E-book reading strategies can help students learn to:

- activate background knowledge
- set a purpose for reading
- identify the main idea
- expand on the main idea with clear, complete explanations
- organize information
- increase comprehension of vocabulary and concepts
- develop the metacognitive process

One of the advantages of using these e-book strategies is that the student reads the e-book and accomplishes all the learning activities within the e-book. No other materials such as paper and pencil are needed, saving on resources and costs. The writing, drawing, and highlighting are all done "in" the book itself.

Nevertheless, the e-book will not be harmed. A student's annotations file can be cleared or renamed, leaving the book like new again—fresh, clean, and without marks—waiting for the next student.

Also, with all the resources in one location, it takes students less time and effort to do the interactions, which increases the likelihood that students will actually complete their work.

The following descriptions of e-book reading strategies are accompanied by steps that apply mainly to MS Reader. At the time of this writing, MS Reader was the e-book format with the greatest level of student interactivity, and therefore was used for the directions in this section. These strategies, however, can be applied to electronic text in many formats. Table 7 describes which e-book reading strategies can be used with the various software formats.

Table 7. E-book Reading Strategies and Formats

E-BOOK READING STRATEGY	MS READER	eREADER	ADOBE READER	WEB BROWSER (HTML)	PLAIN TEXT READER	WORD PROCESSOR
Pre-Reading						
Cover and Title Concept	■	■	■	■		■
Structure of the Text	■	■	■	■	■	■
Word Search	■	■	■	■	■	■
Summary						■
Active and Guided Reading						
Selective Highlighting	■		■*			■
Power Highlighting	■		■*			■
Sticky Notes	■	■	■*			■
Stop and Predict	■	■			■	■
One-Sentence Summary	■	■	■*			■
Reading Log	■	■	■*		■	■
Question Answer Relationship (QAR)	■	■	■*		■	■
Sentence Expansion	■	■	■*		■	■
Literary Element	■	■	■*		■	
Bookmarks	■	■	■*		■	■
Buddy Reading	■		■*			
Concept Mapping	■					■

* *This tool will work if commenting is enabled during creation of the PDF document. If enabled, the Commenting toolbar will be available.*

Pre-Reading Strategies

Pre-reading is an important and useful technique for readers, and for many it becomes an indispensable part of reading for understanding. Pre-reading can be applied to almost any type of reading material, e-book or printed text. The purpose of pre-reading is to develop an overall view of the reading material and therefore be better prepared at the start of reading for depth and understanding. Taking a few minutes in pre-reading can increase reading speed and efficiency. More effective readers are active, not passive, readers. Active readers take time before they begin to read to recall related knowledge, preview the vocabulary and structure, make predictions about the text, establish a purpose, and generate questions to be answered during the reading. The following pre-reading strategies take just a few minutes and can easily be accomplished using e-book technology.

About These Instructions

Unless otherwise noted, the instructions provided in this chapter are specific to MS Reader, but the concepts can easily be applied to other e-book readers. Instructions for HTML books on the Web are provided in parentheses where appropriate.

Cover and Title Concept

This pre-reading activity involves making predictions about an e-book from observing the cover and reading the title. Other information typically found at the front of the book may be viewed as well.

1. Open the e-book.

2. As the book starts, the cover image will display, if there is one. (Some e-books will not have cover images. Either the e-book program doesn't display a cover, or the software used to create the e-book displays a standard software logo as the book cover.)

Figure 5.1. E-book "cover" image and opening page in MS Reader.

 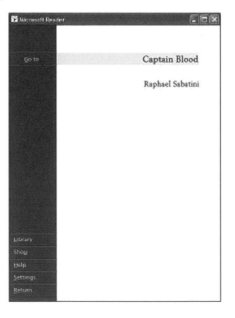

3. To get a general idea of the book, consider the cover image. Go to the cover page to read the title and author of the book (Figure 5.1).

4. You may also want to read, if available, the copyright page.

5. Go to the first page of the text and highlight the title of the work.

6. From the pop-up menu, select **Add Text Note**.

7. In the note space, write a general prediction on what the work will be about.

Structure of the Text

In this activity, a reader observes the table of contents and the structure within the text to learn the book's organization and major features.

1. Open the e-book.

2. Go to the table of contents and read it.

3. Exit the table of contents by clicking or tapping outside the table of contents box.

4. Read the chapter title of the assigned section.

5. Scan the chapter to view the subheadings.

An advantage of e-book technology is that students can usually view the table of contents from any point within the e-book without losing their place.

Figure 5.2. Specific text can be quickly located within an MS Reader e-book.

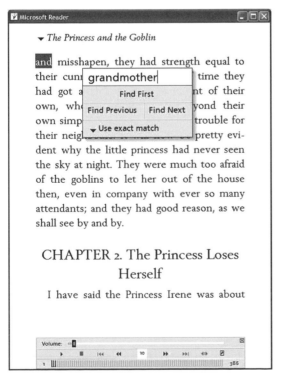

Word Search

This strategy gives the reader a quick glance of the reading material as it relates to a particular word. The reader predicts whether a particular word will be in the text or identifies a word of interest. She or he then searches the text for the word to find it used in context. Another strategy is for a student to search the text for assigned vocabulary to see how it's used. Using this strategy, students can quickly read vocabulary words in context, and can highlight the word as a reminder when later reading the passage.

1. Click on a word in the e-book.

2. From the pop-up menu, choose the **Find...** option. (On a Web page go to the **Edit** menu and choose the **Find** option.)

3. Type in the word you are searching for and choose one of the find options (Figure 5.2).

4. Read the word in context.

5. Search for the word or term again until you reach the end of the book.

To expand this activity into a vocabulary assignment, have the student:

1. Read the passage or sentence that contains the vocabulary word.

2. Select the word and use a linked dictionary to look up the word. Decide which definition is most appropriate.

3. Click outside the definition box to return to the passage.

4. Select the word again, and then from the menu select the option to create a text box.

5. In the text box, write the vocabulary word and the definition that would be the most appropriate for how the word was used in context.

Summary

Many people use summaries to quickly get the main points of documents. Summarizing offers a way to identify and integrate the most important information. Summarizing is extremely important in increasing students' reading comprehension by helping them construct an overall understanding of the text (Oczuks, 2003). It also helps students become proficient readers.

Some word processors, such as Microsoft Word and OpenOffice, have tools that will create a summary, which can be used to quickly preview the reading material. These computer-created summaries may not accurately reflect the content of the work. When a summary is created by computer, students should evaluate and edit it, which helps them recall the important information from the material. Evaluating the computer's summary helps students understand text structures and construct their own summaries.

To create a summary in MS Word:

1. Open the e-book with the word processor. Word can open e-books saved as document (DOC), rich text format (RTF), Web page (HTML), and text (TXT) files.

2. From the **Tools** menu, select **AutoSummarize...** .

3. A pop-up window will appear with the summary options (Figure 5.3). This pop-up provides four ways to summarize and view the summary.

4. Select the first option, **Highlight key points**. This option will return to the text, highlighting what the program considered the important parts and providing the reader with a slider bar that can change the percentage of the material that will be included in the summary. Words that the program doesn't highlight will be left out of the summary report. Readers can use the highlighted text to help them select passages to read or create a new document of just the highlights.

The second option in the AutoSummarize window inserts the summary of the document at the beginning of the document, while the third creates a new document for the summary, and the fourth option replaces the current document with the summary. The percentage of included material can also be selected here.

Figure 5.3. MS Word offers an AutoSummarize pop-up menu.

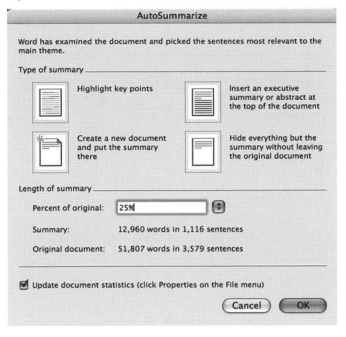

It's best to experiment with the first option to find out the percentage that works for the text material, and then choose one of the other options for placing the new summary. The last percentage where the slider bar was set will automatically be used to create the new summary.

5. Once a percentage has been decided upon, select **AutoSummarize...** again from the **Tools** menu.

6. Now select the option to either create a new document or insert the summary at the beginning of the existing document.

7. You may wish to save and print the created summary file and provide it to students as needed.

AutoSummarize is an easy-to-use tool that will summarize material of any length in a word processor. It can be used to summarize a paragraph, a section, a chapter, or even a whole book. In addition to their utility in pre-reading, these summaries can be used to check a student's reading comprehension and create a reading accommodation for students with special needs by displaying a shorter or simpler form of the text (see chapter 8 for more information on accommodations).

Active and Guided Reading Strategies

Once students have completed any pre-reading assignments, they can move on to active or guided reading. With active or guided reading, readers don't simply "practice" reading; they have a range of objectives to achieve while reading. In pursuing these objectives, students increase their reading comprehension. Readers learn from their reading, and as they progress, learn more about reading itself. Within the metacognitive structure of active or guided reading, students monitor their understanding in an ongoing manner by:

- interacting with the text

- highlighting or marking passages

- making notes about concepts and ideas

- answering questions from the pre-reading or that develop through reading

- writing about the reading

The following reading strategies are well-suited to e-book technology.

Selective Highlighting

This activity is equivalent to underlining or using highlighters with printed text. With e-books, students can use a digital highlighter to select and color portions of text. For example, if students were to identify the main ideas from a reading passage they would:

1. Read the selection.

2. Reread the selection to identify the key ideas.

3. Use the cursor to select the key ideas in the text.

4. From the pop-up menu, choose **Add Highlight** (Figure 5.4).

Figure 5.4. Adding a highlight to selected text in MS Reader.

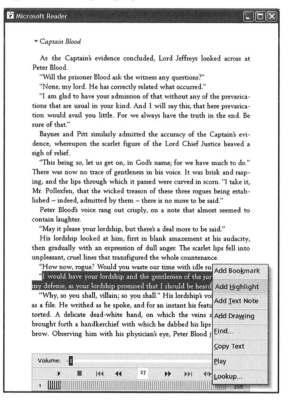

This activity could be expanded by using different highlight colors (see Power Highlighting) or by adding text boxes with notes (see Sticky Notes).

While highlighting is a common activity for many readers, it's often not done well. Unfortunately, many students aren't selective enough about what they highlight, and too often highlight entire sentences, paragraphs, and even pages. The advantage of using digital highlighting is that the text material isn't actually changed. The highlights can easily be removed from the text to correct errors or for use by another student.

Power Highlighting

Power highlighting takes highlighting to a more sophisticated level. The reader uses different highlight colors to identify different aspects of the text, such as the main idea and supporting ideas, opinions and proof, hypothesis and proof, or problems and solutions. In each situation the reader is actively involved in identifying not just key ideas, but how they relate to each other.

To power highlight:

1. Select a portion of the text, such as the main idea.

2. From the pop-up menu, choose **Add Highlight**.

To change the color of the highlight:

1. Select a previously highlighted section of text.

2. From the pop-up menu, choose **Edit Highlight**.

3. From the color menu now on-screen, choose a new highlight color.

Sticky Notes

When using the sticky notes strategy with paper text, a student reads the text and then writes questions, comments, or ideas on a sticky note and places the note in the book. With e-books, as the student reads a passage, he or she types notes linked to specific sections. Digital stickies can't fall out of the book. Plus, the notes are all collected in an annotations file, which the student can access as a hyperlinked list. By viewing the annotations file, a teacher can quickly review a student's compiled e-book notes.

To create a sticky note:

1. Select the portion of the text you wish to comment on or react to.

2. From the pop-up menu, select **Add Text Note**.

3. Type the comment into the text box (Figure 5.5).

4. To finish, click anywhere outside the text box.

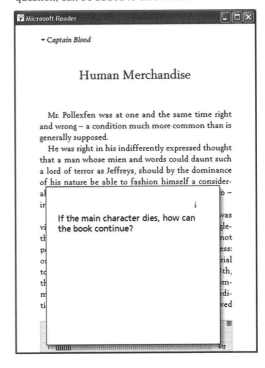

Figure 5.5. Digital sticky notes, such as this question, can be added to an e-book in MS Reader.

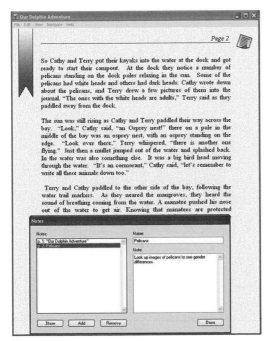

Figure 5.6. A sticky note is added using eReader software.

To create a sticky note using eReader:

- Click on the note icon in the upper right corner or go to the **Navigate** menu and select **Add Note** (Figure 5.6). (In eReader, note names can be changed.)

To create a sticky note using a word processor:

- Go to the **Insert** menu and select **Comment**.

Stop and Predict

With the stop and predict reading strategy, the reader stops reading at a key juncture or event, such as a chapter or section, and then writes a prediction of what will happen next. This strategy is effective for stories, narrative texts, sequences, and cause and effect relationships. With an e-book, the prediction can be associated with a selection of text, and the prediction is written into a text box. These predictions can be viewed in the annotations file.

To make a stop and predict notation, follow the procedure for creating a sticky note.

Figure 5.7. Using the one-sentence summary strategy linked to the last word of a chapter using MS Reader.

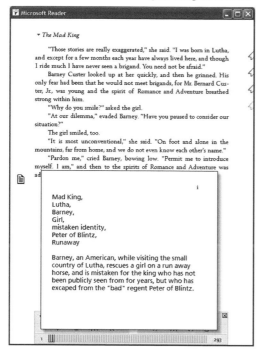

One-Sentence Summary

Another note-taking strategy is the one-sentence summary. In this case a reader creates a linked note in a text box at the end of a chapter, passage, or paragraph, then writes a list of key words from the section. The reader then crafts a single sentence that summarizes the reading, incorporating the key words (Figure 5.7).

To add a one-sentence summary, follow the procedure for creating a sticky note.

Reading Log

When creating a reading log, the student reads a section or chapter, then creates a text box and writes a free-response entry without any specific content focus for about 5–10 minutes, depending on the student's age and the topic. With the free response technique, a student can write about feelings, thoughts, questions, reactions, or personal experiences. For e-books this activity is an adaptation of the sticky note:

1. Select the last word from the section.

2. Create an associated text box following the procedure for adding a sticky note.

3. For a designated period of time, write a free-response associated with the reading that was just completed.

Question Answer Relationship

Developed by Taffy Raphael (1986) as a strategy to increase reading comprehension, the Question Answer Relationship or QAR strategy has students develop questions about the material that was read. The questions developed are both literal (Right There and Think and Search) and creative (Author and You and On My Own). Right There questions are ones that can be answered from words found in a single sentence. Think and Search questions are also in the text, but are spread throughout the reading passage. Answers to Author and You questions aren't found within the text, but relate to the text's content. On My Own questions don't even require reading the passage; instead, they're based on the reader's prior knowledge or background. With e-books this strategy is an adaptation of adding a sticky note (Figure 5.8).

1. Highlight a passage or the last sentence of the passage.

2. Create a text box following the procedure for adding a sticky note.

3. In the text box write the following terms, each on a different line:

   ■ Right There

   ■ Think and Search

- Author and You
- On My Own

4. Write a question that relates to the passage after each category.

Sentence Expansion

Sentence expansion is a vocabulary activity in which students revise text with different vocabulary (Figure 5.9). This activity is effective for analyzing texts that are relatively old, because language usage will have shifted since their publication.

1. Highlight or select a descriptive sentence from the e-book.

2. Copy the text.

3. Select the sentence again and create an associated text box following the procedure for adding a sticky note.

4. Paste the sentence into the text box twice.

5. Edit the second version of the sentence, replacing the existing words with words that are easier to understand or more interesting.

Figure 5.8. Using QAR in a text box in MS Reader.

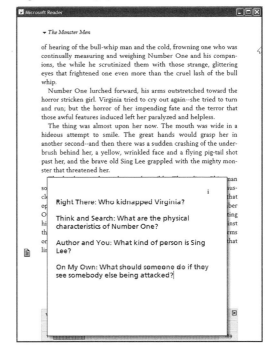

Figure 5.9. An example of sentence expansion using MS Reader.

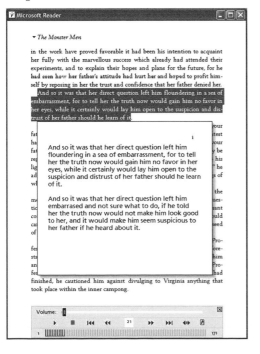

Literary Element

Literary element is a reading strategy in which students make comments about how a text is actually written, not just what occurs in the text. Students can make notes about character development, descriptive words, actions, or other elements.

Expanding this strategy, readers can also create digital drawings of a passage in an e-book (Figure 5.10). The drawings can be toggled on and off to avoid disruption during reading. The student's work is hyperlinked to the associated portion of the text and can be accessed from the annotations file.

To add a literary element comment, follow the procedure for creating a sticky note. To add a literary element drawing, select a portion of text. From the pop-up menu, select **Add Drawing**.

Figure 5.10. A student's literary element drawing based on a passage in Edgar Rice Burroughs' *The Monster Men.*

Bookmarks

Using digital bookmarks, a student can quickly jump to different locations within the text. This strategy can be used to identify passages that display plot or character development as well as to flag other key elements such as steps, timelines, or sequences. Depending on the e-book program, it may be possible to change the bookmark colors to group similar or associated passages.

To add a bookmark:

1. Select the text associated with the key element.

2. From the pop-up menu, select **Add Bookmark**. The bookmark flag that appears on the side will be associated with the selected text, not the page number. To return to the text, click it.

To change the color of a bookmark:

1. Click on the bookmark.

2. Select the option to **Change Color**.

3. Select the desired color.

Unlike bookmarks in printed books, these digital bookmarks will never fall out. Increasing the text size won't affect the location of the bookmark because it's linked to a selected portion of the text, not a page number.

Bookmarks in eReader

The eReader program will create bookmarks associated with pages. The bookmark's position will change if the display change affects the page numbering in the book. Once created, a bookmark image will appear on the marked page, but there will be no "icon set" showing all the bookmarks (Figure 5.11). Instead, you can access eReader bookmarks by going to the **Navigate** menu and selecting **Bookmarks**, and then choosing the hyperlinked page for the particular bookmark you want.

Figure 5.11. Pages are easily bookmarked in eReader.

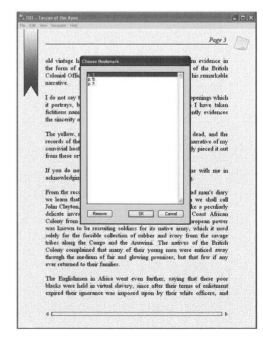

Buddy Reading

Normally during buddy reading, pairs of students read and assist each other as they read, taking turns reading aloud or in unison. They stop periodically to discuss the story with each other. With the application of text-to-speech technology, it's possible to use the computer as a reader's buddy, a form of self-buddy reading. Using this format, a student can read with or take turns with the reading device, or use the e-book program to read specific words that the student may have trouble with. While this form of read-aloud lacks the discussion and interpersonal aspect, it does present the text to the student through both visual and auditory methods. See chapters 6 and 8 for more information on using text-to-speech applications.

An adaptation that can make this more like buddy reading is for the student to first listen to the text-to-speech reading of the passage and add a text box, writing a summary and questions for clarification. This summary could then be shared with other readers or the instructor.

Figure 5.12. A character map can be created in MS Reader by adding a drawing over the text.

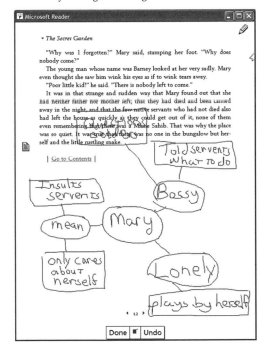

Concept Mapping

Concept, content, or mind maps are graphic organizers used to show relationships among different pieces of information. Concept maps support student understanding by showing the organization of the topic in a visual manner. Any form of concept or content mapping is possible with an e-book program that allows drawing as a form of annotation (Figure 5.12). If the reader can't easily manipulate a mouse, creating concept maps within e-books can be made easier using a tablet computer, handheld reader, or other device that uses a pen or stylus for input.

When including concept maps in an e-book, it's best to create blank pages for the reader to draw on (Figure 5.13). If blank pages can't be inserted, it's still possible to draw the map on top of the text. The graphic display can be turned on or off to keep the drawing from distracting the reader.

The advantage of using digital drawing to create concept maps is that the text material isn't actually changed; the drawings can easily be removed from the text to correct errors or to allow use by another student.

To create a concept map in an e-book:

1. Provide students with a topic from the reading for the map, or a type of drawing (such as a character concept map, timeline, or Venn diagram).

2. From the pop-up menu, students select **Add Drawing**.

3. Students create the concept map by drawing and writing with the mouse or stylus.

A good strategy is for a student to add bookmarks to flag the beginning and ending of the passage, then read the passage, highlighting important or relevant sections. At the end of the chapter, the student develops the concept map, including the elements she has identified.

Conclusion

Today's students live in the Digital Age, and we as educators should integrate technology into our students' literacy experiences. As the concept of literacy transforms to embrace technology, so too must the strategies that our students use to achieve literacy. As teachers provide a wide range of interactive literacy experiences, students will gain a greater appreciation for reading along with skills to analyze, understand, and interact with text. Providing students with technology experiences and tools for reading strategies should be part of a balanced literacy program.

Online Resources

Software

Adobe Reader: www.adobe.com

eReader Pro: www.ereader.com/product/browse/software

Firefox (Web browser that can display Web-based e-books): www.firefox.com

Internet Explorer (Web browser that can display Web-based e-books): www.microsoft. com/downloads

MS Reader: www.microsoft.com/reader

MS Word: www.microsoft.com/word

Netscape (Web browser that can display Web-based e-books): http://channels.netscape. com/ns/browsers/default.jsp

OpenOffice (Word processor that displays DOC, TXT, and HTML documents): www.openoffice.org

E-book Information

DrsCavanaugh (e-books in education information): www.drscavanaugh.org/ebooks

eBRS, e-Book Reading Strategies (reading strategies applied to digital text): www.drscavanaugh.org/ebooks/ebrs/intro.htm

International Reading Association: www.reading.org

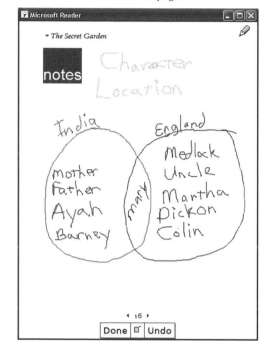

Figure 5.13. A Venn diagram has been drawn in MS Reader on a blank e-book page.

References

Bigum, C., & Lankshear, C. (1998, July 7). *Literacies and technologies in school settings: Findings from the field.* Keynote address presented to the ALEA/ATEA National Conference, Canberra, Australia. Retrieved June 2005 from http://www.schools.ash.org.au/litweb/bigum.html

Gee, J. P. (1989). Literacy, discourse, and linguistics: An introduction. *Journal of Education, 17,* 5–25.

Kress, G. (2003). *Literacy in the new media age.* London: Routledge.

National Institute for Literacy. (1991). What is the NALS? In *The State of Literacy in America: Estimates at the Local, State, and National Levels.* Retrieved September 2004 from http://www.nifl.gov/reders/!intro.htm#C

Oczuks, L. (2003). *Reciprocal teaching at work: Strategies for improving reading comprehension.* Newark, DE: International Reading Association.

Raphael, T. (1986). Teaching Question and Answer Relationships, revisited. *Reading Teacher, 39*(6) 516–522.

Semali, L. (2001, November). Defining new literacies in curricular practice. *Reading Online, 5*(4). Retrieved October 2004 from http://www.readingonline.org/newliteracies/lit_index.asp?HREF=semali1/index.html

Chapter 6

Picture Books and Read-Alouds

While we may think of picture books as being designed for beginning readers, this isn't always the case. Research has found that picture books can be effective and appropriate reading tools for everyone. After all, how many of us have some form of "picture book" on the coffee table?

Students should be given the opportunity to select the texts they want to read, including easy texts (Ivey, 1999), which allow them to practice reading with greater fluency. Numerous Web sites offer picture e-books. Some incorporate multimedia into the book's presentation, making them even more appealing to today's students.

Another useful format is read-alouds, which is an excellent application for e-books. To help students improve reading fluency, teachers should provide oral reading opportunities and monitor students as they read out loud (National Institute for Literacy, 2002). Often we as educators don't have the time to read aloud to every student; luckily e-books can read aloud to students whenever students want. A wide range of read-aloud technologies allow students to hear books or other materials read aloud to them. Formats include text-to-speech programs, Flash books, Internet video, and audio books.

Why Picture Books?

A well-organized, extensive classroom library includes all genres of literature, including magazines, comic books, and even picture books. Picture books can be an important element in helping maintain student interest in extending reading (Worthy, 1996, 2000).

Picture books are more than just children's literature. They are themselves literature. A picture storybook or illustrated book delivers its tale in two narratives. The pictures and text work interdependently in a joining of verbal and visual arts (Benedict & Carlisle, 1992).

Neal and Moore (1991) developed five reasons why teachers should use picture books with more than just young students:

1. The themes of many picture books have universal value and will appeal to all age levels.

2. Some of the best picture books may have been missed when the students were younger or may have been published since they were children. How many of us read Janell Cannon's *Stellaluna* as children?

3. Many topics and issues brought up in picture books demand a mature level of understanding that young children may not possess.

4. Picture books are typically short and can be incorporated into a single class period. (Most picture books are only 24 to 48 pages, a brief length that won't discourage even beginning readers.)

5. Our visually oriented society has conditioned students to use pictures as scaffolding or aids to comprehension.

Picture Books Throughout the Curriculum

Within a class, picture books should be selected to help support the curriculum and relate to instruction. Not only are they effective tools for reading, they can be a perfect tool for illustrating topics in science, the humanities, and art, to name a few.

NASA, for example, produces two online picture books that discuss remote sensing through the context of a story. One of these texts, *Echo the Bat*, is also published in paper format by the Government Printing Office, probably the only "pop-up" book the U.S. government prints (Figure 6.1).

The U.S. military Web site on the Korean War also publishes an online picture book, titled *Peacebound Trains*, by Haemi Balgassi and Chris K. Soentpiet. *Peacebound Trains* is the story of a young girl who escapes from Seoul with her grandmother just before the war (Figure 6.2). This online picture book could be used as a resource for teaching about history, culture, and geography.

The boxes on the next pages illustrate how each of these books can be used in the curriculum to meet subject-area standards.

Figure 6.1. NASA's *Echo the Bat* online story is accompanied by a teacher's guide, lab activities, and worksheets.

Figure 6.2. Korean War Memorial's Web site includes the story *Peacebound Trains* as well as a teacher's guide with reading and interdisciplinary activities.

Echo the Bat
http://imagers.gsfc.nasa.gov

Echo the Bat can be used as an Earth science education resource for the introduction of remote sensing and satellite imagery. The Echo the Bat Web site provides a teacher's guide with lessons, lab activities, and worksheets to help students understand light and the electromagnetic spectrum. *Echo the Bat* and its associated Web site can be used to teach the science standards listed below.

Grade Level: K–8

Subject: Science

National Science Education Standards, Grades 5–8

Physical Science

Content Standard B: Transfer of Energy

- Light interacts with matter by transmission (including refraction), absorption, or scattering (including reflection). To see an object, light from that object—emitted by or scattered from it—must enter the eye.

- The Sun is a major source of energy for changes on the Earth's surface. The Sun loses energy by emitting light. A tiny fraction of that light reaches the Earth, transferring energy from the Sun to the Earth. The Sun's energy arrives as a light with a range of wavelengths, consisting of visible light, infrared, and ultraviolet radiation.

Life Science

Content Standard C: Populations and Ecosystems

- A population consists of all individuals of a species that occur together at a given place and time. All populations living together and the physical factors with which they interact compose an ecosystem.

- Populations of organisms can be categorized by the function they serve in an ecosystem. Plants and some micro-organisms are producers—they make their own food. All animals, including humans, are consumers, which obtain food by eating other organisms. Decomposers, primarily bacteria and fungi, are consumers that use waste materials and dead organisms for food. Food webs identify the relationships among producers, consumers, and decomposers in an ecosystem.

Science and Technology

Content Standard E: Understandings about Science and Technology.

- Science and technology are reciprocal. Science helps drive technology, as it addresses questions that demand more sophisticated instruments and provides principles for better instrumentation and technique. Technology is essential to science, because it provides instruments and techniques that enable observations of objects and phenomena that are otherwise unobservable due to factors such as quantity, distance, location, size, and speed. Technology also provides tools for investigations, inquiry, and analysis.

Science in Personal and Social Perspectives

Content Standard F: Populations, Resources, and Environments

- When an area becomes overpopulated, the environment will become degraded due to the increased use of resources.

- Causes of environmental degradation and resource depletion vary from region to region from country to country.

Standards are reprinted with permission from National Science Education Standards, copyright © 1996 by the National Academy of Sciences, courtesy of the National Academies Press, Washington, D.C.

Peacebound Trains
http://korea50.army.mil/pacebound/

Peacebound Trains can be used to introduce social studies students to concepts of the Korean War, refugees, multigenerational families, military families, and forms of transportation. The Korean War Commemoration Web site provides a teacher's guide with reading and interdisciplinary activities for students. *Peacebound Trains* and its associated Web site can be used to teach the social studies standards listed below.

Grade Level: 9–12

Subject: U.S. or World History

National Council for the Social Studies Thematic Strands

High School

II. **Time, Continuity, and Change**

b. Students apply key concepts such as time, chronology, causality, change, conflict, and complexity to explain, analyze, and show connections among patterns of historical change and continuity.

VI. **Power, Authority, and Governance**

e. Students compare different political systems (their ideologies, structure, institutions, processes, and political cultures) with that of the United States, and identify representative political leaders from selected historical and contemporary settings.

g. Students evaluate the role of technology in communications, transportation, information-processing, weapons development, or other areas as it contributes to or helps resolve conflicts.

Middle Grades

II. **Time, Continuity, and Change**

b. Students identify and use key concepts such as chronology, change, conflict, and complexity to explain, analyze, and show connections among patterns of historical change and continuity.

III. **People, Places, and Environments**

a. Students elaborate mental maps of locales, regions, and the world that demonstrate understanding of relative location, direction, size, and shape.

b. Students create, interpret, use, and distinguish various representations of the Earth, such as maps, globes, and photographs.

d. Students estimate distance, calculate scale, and distinguish other geographic relationships such as population density and spatial distribution patterns.

VI. **Power, Authority, and Governance**

g. Students describe and analyze the role of technology in communications, transportation, information-processing, weapons development, or other areas as it contributes to or helps resolve conflicts.

VIII. **Science, Technology, and Society**

a. Students examine and describe the influence of culture on scientific and technological choices and advancement, such as in transportation, medicine, and warfare.

Standards are reprinted with permission from Expectations of Excellence—Curriculum Standards for Social Studies, published by the National Council for the Social Studies. Copyright © 1994.

Foreign Language and Multicultural Picture Books

Numerous picture books available online support foreign language instruction and multicultural studies. Through such books, students can see the world from different viewpoints, and learn about other cultures and languages. For instance, the site Renny Yaniar's Children's Stories and Folktales from Indonesia (www.geocities.com/kesumawijaya) offers original stories and Indonesian folktales, in both Indonesian and English languages.

Books from specialized Web sites such as Renny Yaniar's, as well as from online multicultural libraries, provide foreign language instructors with an extensive instructional resource. A common problem in these classrooms is finding supporting reading materials in the target language. How many local bookstores carry books written in multiple foreign languages? Using online resources gives instructors books for just about every foreign language course taught in schools.

These books also provide exceptional scaffolds for ESL students. Through online digital libraries, even novice readers should be able to find high-interest, age-appropriate picture books at their reading level, without a daunting length. Furthermore, these books can be used to support the initial language, offering something students could read "from home" or share with others as works from their homelands. Consequently, the books support two facets of reading development for ESL students: they support reading in English as well as growth and maintenance of the initial language.

Social studies curricula can also benefit from these books. For example, multicultural books can be used in a social studies class to study cultures, history, and geography. Students select a book, review it, and locate its country of origin on a map, and then discuss the culture within a literature circle.

The International Children's Digital Library

One of the best multicultural picture book libraries that I have found is the International Children's Digital Library (Figure 6.3). The ICDL is a jointly funded project of the National Science Foundation and the Institute for Museum and Library Services being constructed by the University of Maryland/College Park and the Internet Archive. Within the ICDL site, users can search for books by title, topic, publication date, language, or author.

While the goal of the ICDL is to have more than 10,000 books in more than 100 languages placed online in the next five years, teachers, librarians, parents, and students don't have to wait, as the site already hosts more than 300 books in 23 languages. This includes more than 175 books in English, some of which are considered classics, such as Jane Cowen-Fletcher's *It Takes a Village*, Yolen and Teague's *How Do Dinosaurs Say Goodnight?*, and Molly Bang's award-winning *When Sophie Gets Angry—Really, Really Angry....*

Figure 6.3. The International Children's Digital Library book searching page can quickly locate books in 23 languages.

Reproduced with permission of ICDL.

The other languages represented in the ICDL range from Arabic to Vietnamese and Maori to Russian, and several books are in more than one language, such as English and Spanish.

Meeting Standards with Online Picture Books

Online picture books, such as those from ICDL, can provide a starting point for student story-writing, supply additional high-interest reading, and engage students in multicultural reading and experiences. Consider how educators can use ICDL with students to meet state and national education standards. For example Florida's Sunshine State Standards (Florida State Board of Education, 1996) could be met using ICDL e-books in two sample standard areas: reading and foreign language.

Consider the following scenario: Ms. Cailin's Spanish class is practicing translation. She wants to give her students a more authentic experience by having them translate existing literature at their Spanish ability level. Ms. Cailin located several electronic versions of children's picture books from ICDL to use with her class. Using a video projector connected to her computer, she displays the pages of the text on the screen and then demonstrates the translating process by writing the translation on the board. Next, she opens another children's book and has the class attempt to translate each of the pages. As part of a homework assignment, students are asked to translate a specific page from another book, which will then be read aloud while it is being displayed the next day. Through this activity, Ms. Cailin meets the following standards.

Language Arts

■ PK–12: Strand Reading; Standard 2: The student constructs meaning from a wide range of texts. (LA.A.2.1) (LA.A.2.2) (LA.A.2.3) (LA.A.2.4)

■ 6–8: Strand Writing; Benchmark 4: Uses electronic technology including databases and software to gather information and communicate new knowledge. (LA.B.2.3)

■ 9–12: Strand Writing; Benchmark 4: Selects and uses a variety of electronic media, such as the Internet, information services and desktop publishing software programs to create, revise, retrieve, and verify information. (LA.B.2.4)

Online Picture Books as Big Books

E-books can be adapted for use in the classroom as digital "big books." Obtaining printed teacher big books and their associated student small books can be an expensive prospect, and titles are limited. By using an LCD overhead panel, a video projector, or a large-screen television connected to a computer, a teacher may display a picture book to the whole class as part of an instructional reading activity or as an example of writing, culture, or art (Figure 6.4).

Not only does displaying an e-book as a digital big book save the cost of purchasing a large version, these e-books have the added advantage of being available to students for outside reading.

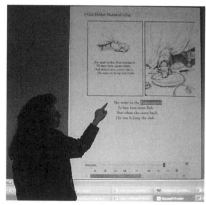

Figure 6.4. A teacher uses an MS Reader digital big book for instruction.

Foreign Languages

■ PK–12: Strand Communication; Standard 2: The student understands and interprets written and spoken language on a variety of topics. (FL.A.2.1) (FL.A.2.2) (FL.A.2.3) (FL.A.2.4)

■ PK–12: Strand Culture; Standard 1: The student understands the relationship between the perspectives and products of culture studied and uses this knowledge to recognize cultural practices. (FL.B.1.1) (FL.B.1.2) (FL.B.1.3) (FL.B.1.4)

■ PK–12: Strand Connections; Standard 2: The student acquires information and perspectives that are available only through the foreign language and within the target culture. (FL.C.2.1) (FL.C.2.2) (FL.C.2.3) (FL.C.2.4)

These standards are just a few examples that could be met throughout the PK–12 program through the use of the ICDL. The books in this online digital library could be used at all grade levels to assist in the teaching of science, social studies, language arts, art, and even math.

Why Read-Alouds?

We know that it's important to read aloud to students. Anderson, Hiebert, Scott, and Wilkinson, in their 1985 report for the U.S. Department of Education's Commission on Reading, *Becoming a Nation of Readers*, state that "the single most important activity for building the knowledge required for eventual success in reading is reading aloud to children" (p. 23). Similarly, the Family Literacy Foundation (2002) states that studies show one of the most important things that can be done in preparing children for success in school and reading is to read aloud to them: reading aloud helps build listening skills, vocabulary, memory, and language skills and helps children learn information about the world around them.

According to several researchers, including Jim Trelease (1995) and Carbo, Dunn, and Dunn (1986), a balanced school reading program should include daily read-alouds to students. Some of the positive effects of reading aloud to students that are supported through research are an awareness of language and an appreciation of literature in all forms. Reading aloud can increase a student's language acquisition and influence the child to become a better reader. Just hearing a book read aloud can improve a child's ability to listen for periods of time, increasing attention spans (Montgomery County Public Schools Department of Academic Programs, 1999).

To get the most out of read-alouds, according to Reutzel (2001) and Daye (2003), teachers should:

■ use books of high student interest that reflect the cultures and languages of the students

■ involve students in choosing the books to be read

■ choose appropriate text levels that are above the reading level of the students

■ control the length of time, usually 10–15 minutes

■ expose students to a wide range of materials, not just books

■ vary group size, not just whole class, but also small groups or one-to-one

■ have students make predictions about the text and recall prior knowledge

■ make the reading environment comfortable

Teresa Daye (2003) also points out that "reading aloud to students has proven effective in secondary schools as well as in elementary schools."

E-books as Read-Alouds

Often we as educators don't have the time to read aloud to every student, but e-books can read aloud to students whenever students want. A wide range of read-aloud technologies allow students to hear books or other materials read aloud to them through some form of e-book. It's almost like having a guest reader visit your class to read to one or a few students, anytime you want.

E-book technology can assist teachers and students in integrating or expanding read-alouds. Students can use a wide range of read-aloud technologies to hear books or other materials read aloud to them through some form of e-book. Reading to students can help them understand the purpose of the printed word, expand their vocabulary beyond what they can read for themselves, acquire the background to recognize new words they are decoding, and learn the connection between the spoken and printed word. In summarizing research done on using technology to read aloud to students, Ernest Balajthy (2005) identifies the benefits that the technology has brought to many students, such as increased word identification, improved attention to text, and increased comprehension. In a summary of research and results presented by Recorded Books (2004), audio support of books assists students in developing their reading fluency and comprehension.

[**Lesson**Idea]

Audio Book Library

Ask students and parents to donate audio books that they have listened to and create an audio book library for a class or school. The use of audio text with print text has been found to increase learning by 38%.

Most libraries today have e-books as books on tape and CD, but instructors shouldn't be limited by a library's current collection. The Internet abounds with e-book read-aloud resource materials for all grade levels and subjects. E-book read-aloud formats include text-to-speech programs, Flash books, Internet video, and audio books.

Text-to-Speech Programs

Using text materials from the Internet and a text-to-speech program, any student can have a book read aloud by a computer. The most recent text-to-speech programs don't just read word by word, but also look at the sentence for context, such as past, present, or future tense of words. They vary the tonality of the speech to avoid monotone, and they use standard speech structures such as tone changes for questions. Some text-to-speech engines will also read in other languages, enabling an e-book written in French to be read with French speech, for instance (see chapter 4 for more foreign language applications).

Any of the hundreds of free online libraries can provide text that a text-to-speech program then reads aloud. E-book programs for such read-alouds include Adobe Reader and Microsoft Reader. Both programs are free and available for desktop and handheld computers.

MS Reader (www.microsoft.com/reader), which displays books in LIT format, has a text-to-speech engine that reads aloud with synchronized highlighting of the text.

Adobe Reader (www.adobe.com/products/acrobat/readstep2.html), which displays books in PDF format, comes equipped with a feature called Read Out Loud (Figure 6.5).

Figure 6.5. Adobe Reader's Read Out Loud feature can be downloaded from the Adobe site.

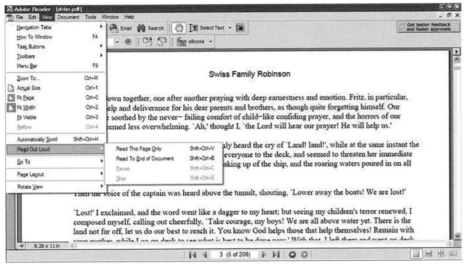

Adobe product screenshot reprinted with permission from Adobe Systems Incorporated.

Flash Books

Several very good children's picture books are read-aloud e-books in Flash format, accessible through the Internet. Most of the books in Flash format are for the younger or emergent reader. With this format, a Web browser uses a plug-in program to display the text while a human reader's recorded voice reads the text. Flash books are displayed on screen one page at a time. The user clicks to advance to the next page.

While a special program is needed to create Flash material, the reader only needs to install the free Flash plug-in. It can be downloaded for no charge from Macromedia at www.macromedia.com/downloads/.

One of the best Flash sites for read-aloud storybooks is RIF Reading Planet (www.rif.org/readingplanet/content/read_aloud_stories.mspx), sponsored by Reading is Fundamental (Figure 6.6). The Scholastic organization also has a site with picture read-aloud books about Clifford the Big Red Dog (http://teacher.scholastic.com/clifford1/). Here children make choices about what happens and then hear the new story read aloud.

Figure 6.6. The RIF Reading Planet site offers children's books in Flash format.

© *RIF Reading Planet.*

Figure 6.7. *Somebody Loves You, Mr. Hatch* is read aloud in a video window by actor Hector Elizondo at the Storyline Online Web site.

© BookPALS, a program for the Screen Actors Guild Foundation.

Internet Video

While we usually think of video as playing on the TV with a tape or DVD, you can also receive and play video with a computer. Educators and students can find on the Internet video recordings of people reading picture books. The person reading the book, and specific pages in the book, are usually included in the presentation. Read-aloud books in this format are usually for younger and emergent readers.

Storyline Online from the Screen Actors Guild Foundation and BookPALS (http://bookpals.net/storyline/) offers 11 video presentations of stories read by professional, well-known actors. At the site, choose the book desired, and select the video format and display size. The book video will be streamed to the computer. To see the e-book, press the play button, just like on the VCR (Figure 6.7).

Audio Books

Audio books have been around for a long time, from 78 rpm records to LPs to today's iPods playing MP3 files. These books use a recorded audio format such as cassette tape, CD, or MP3. A person reads the text, but the text isn't displayed. While popular books can be purchased as audio books from bookstores, books used in schools can be purchased in audio format from the company Recorded Books (www.recorded-books.com), which offers books on tape and CD.

Figure 6.8. The Audio Book for Free site offers unabridged versions of texts.

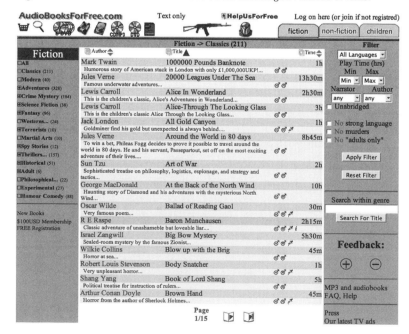

Several Web sites, such as Wired for Books (www.wiredforbooks.org) and Audio Books for Free (www.audiobooksforfree.com), offer unabridged versions of texts students can listen to while they read along on a text copy (Figure 6.8).

These sites aren't limited to children's literature. Audio Books for Free has a few hundred books that can be downloaded and played on a computer or transferred to an MP3 player. Titles include classics such as *The Phantom of the Opera*, *The Prisoner of Zenda*, and

Figure 6.9. The Wired for Books site offers classics as audio books, such as *Alice's Adventures in Wonderland*.

© Wired for Books. Kit DeBerry, illustrator.

The Wind in the Willows. Wired for Books offers interviews with authors and titles such as *A Christmas Carol*, *Alice in Wonderland*, and the Beatrix Potter stories, along with short stories and excerpts from the classics (Figure 6.9). The BookPALS organization also produces audio books that are available by phone. The story offered changes about every two weeks.

Conclusion

Picture books should not be overlooked as a valuable educational aid, for students of all ages and in virtually all subject areas. Read-alouds are also an important resource to build listening skills, memory, and language skills. The availability of e-books makes both of these resources accessible and useful in new and exciting ways.

Online Resources

Audio and Video Books

Audio Books for Free (e-book library/bookstore with MP3 audio books): www.audiobooksforfree.com/screen_main.asp

BookPALS (streaming video e-books: QuickTime, Windows Media, RealPlayer): http://bookpals.net/storyline/

Children's Storybooks Online (Flash format): www.magickeys.com/books/

Clifford's Interactive Storybooks (Flash format): http://teacher.scholastic.com/clifford1/

DreamBox StoryBox (Flash format): www.dreambox.com/storybox/

Internet Archive (audio files and e-books): www.archive.org

Random House Books: www.randomhouse.com
This site provides excerpts from audio books in RealPlayer format. Check the Book Browse section for a category listing.

Recorded Books (audio book sales for schools): www.recordedbooks.com

RIF Reading Planet (Flash format): www.rif.org/readingplanet/content/
read_aloud_stories.mspx

Wired for Books (RealPlayer audio books): www.wiredforbooks.org

Picture Books

International Children's Digital Library: www.icdlbooks.org

NASA's Echo the Bat and Amelia the Pigeon: http://imagers.gsfc.nasa.gov
A hardcopy of Echo the Bat can be ordered from the Government Printing Office at
http://bookstore.gpo.gov/educators/environment.html.

Peacebound Trains (picture book from the Korean War Memorial site): http://korea50.
army.mil/pacebound/

Renny Yaniar's Children's Stories and Folktales from Indonesia: www.geocities.com/
kesumawi0jaya

Software

Adobe Reader (e-book program with text-to-speech application): www.adobe.com

Macromedia Flash (special player program): www.macromedia.com/downloads

MS Reader (e-book program with text-to-speech application): www.microsoft.com/
reader/

References

Anderson, R. C., Hiebert, E. H., Scott, J. A., & Wilkinson, I. A. G. (1985). *Becoming a nation of readers: The report of the commission on reading.* Washington, DC: U. S. Department of Education.

Balajthy, E. (2005, January/February). Text-to-speech software for helping struggling readers. *Reading Online, 8*(4). Retrieved May 2005 from http://www.readingonline.org/articles/art_index.asp?HREF=balajthy2/index.html

Benedict, S., & Carlisle, L. (Eds.). (1992). *Beyond words: Picture books for older readers and writers.* Portsmouth, NH: Heinemann.

Carbo, M., Dunn, R., & Dunn, K. (1986). *Teaching students to read through their individual learning styles.* Englewood Cliffs, NJ: Allyn & Bacon.

Daye, T. J. (2003). *Read-aloud: Research briefs.* Retrieved October 2004 from http://www.ncpublicschools.org/schoolimprovement/effective/briefs/readaloud?

Family Literacy Foundation. (2002). *Why read aloud with children?* Retrieved October 2004 from http://www.read2kids.org

Florida State Board of Education. (1996). *Sunshine state standards.* Retrieved October 2004 from http://www.firn.edu/doe/menu/sss.htm

Ivey, G. (1999). Reflections on teaching struggling middle school readers. *Journal of Adolescent & Adult Literacy, 42*(5), 372–381.

Montgomery County Public Schools Department of Academic Programs. (1999). *Early literacy guide.* Retrieved October 2004 from http://www.mcps.k12.md.us/curriculum/english/read_aloud.html

National Academy of Sciences, National Academies Press. (1996). *National science education standards.* Washington, DC: Author.

National Council for the Social Studies. (1994). *Expectations of excellence: Curriculum standards for social studies*. Silver Springs, MD: Author.

National Institute for Literacy. (2002). *Put reading first: The research building blocks for teaching children to read*. Retrieved August 2005 from http://www.nifl.gov

Neal, J. C., & Moore, K. (1991). The Very Hungry Caterpillar meets Beowulf in secondary classrooms. *Journal of Reading, 35*(4), 290–296.

Recorded Books. (2004). *Recorded books work: Research & results*. Prince Frederick, MD: Author.

Reutzel, D. R. (2001, May). New thinking on READ-ALOUD. *Instructor*. Retrieved October 2004 from http://www.findarticles.com/p/articles/mi_m0STR/is_8_110/ai_74826102

Trelease, J. (1995). *The read-aloud handbook*. New York: Penguin Books.

Worthy, J. (1996). Removing barriers to voluntary reading for reluctant readers: The role of school and classroom libraries. *Language Arts, 73*, 483–492.

Worthy, J. (2000). Teachers' and students' suggestions for motivating middle-school students to read. In T. Shanahan & F. V. Brown (Eds.), *The 49th yearbook of the National Reading Conference* (pp. 441–451). Chicago: National Reading Conference.

Chapter 7 — E-books and the Reluctant Reader

Reading difficulties frustrate educators and students. It is estimated, from a national longitudinal study, that more than 17% of young children will encounter a problem learning to read (National Center to Improve the Tools of Educators [NCITE], 1996). Additionally, the National Assessment of Education Progress (NAEP) report of 2001 indicated that all schools in the United States have children who are failing the task of learning to read. The report stated that 38% of fourth-graders, 26% of eighth-graders, and 23% of 12th-graders were reading at a "below basic" level in 1998.

Difficulties that students have with reading can often be addressed with e-books. Because reading is a basic component of most educational activities, providing alternative formats and supports is necessary to reach all students. For many students, just a small reading support can make a big difference, a support that e-books can provide.

For example, a student with special needs that I worked with had trouble reading with speed and comprehension. After simply changing the background of the text to yellow, her reading speed more than doubled and she showed a marked increase in comprehension—in just the first day of using e-book technology.

The availability of books is another key factor in reading achievement. Countries scoring higher in reading provide students with greater access to books (Elley, 1992). Additional data support this need for book access by students. Krashen (1995) found a positive correlation between reading comprehension scores and the number of books per student in school libraries.

Student readers can be generally classified into three broad categories: strategic readers, reluctant readers, and remedial readers (West-Christy, 2003).

Strategic readers. These students effectively use reading strategies that allow comprehension of a text on or above the instructional reading level.

Reluctant readers. These students usually can read any material in which they are interested, but have text difficulties and few reading strategies.

Remedial readers. These readers typically read several grade levels below their peers, with limited vocabulary and few reading strategies.

Many of the activities that encourage good readers can actually discourage nonreaders by intimidating them and confirming their negative feelings toward reading (Beers & Samuels, 1998). In summarizing the reluctant reader, Pritchard (n.d.) further identifies two distinct groups: students with learning difficulties and students who are nonvoluntary readers.

All of these students, the reluctant and remedial readers, need additional tools to scaffold their reading. E-books can be one of those tools.

Five Techniques

Janice West-Christy (2003) identifies the following five techniques for assisting struggling reluctant and remedial readers. Of these techniques, e-books can clearly support four of them, and offer new opportunities for achieving the fifth (pre-reading techniques).

Offer a wide range of reading materials. A classroom with even a single computer and an Internet connection can make thousands of additional books available to students.

Incorporate large-print materials. Most e-book programs will allow users to vary the font size and make enlarged or "large-print" displays, with a few clicks of the mouse.

Engage multiple modalities. Many e-book readers provide a read-aloud feature with synchronized highlighting to engage reading in multiple modalities.

Teach important vocabulary. Using e-book readers with interactive dictionaries can provide just-in-time learning for new vocabulary.

Use pre-reading techniques. While most e-books don't have pre-reading techniques built in, a teacher could use an e-book's note-taking tool to provide questions and guidance for pre-reading and active reading strategies.

Offer a Wide Range of Reading Materials

According to Richard Allington (2001, 2005), one of the best ways for students to become better readers is to read more. Students need access to books that entice them, therefore attracting them to reading. Expanding the classroom and school library can easily be accomplished with readily available e-books. Free online libraries offer a range of titles. Even more are available for purchase from electronic bookstores. With tens of thousands of e-books available through the Web, students can drastically increase the chances of finding something of interest to them to read. See part 3 for more on digital libraries.

Educators can empower students by allowing them to determine their own reading selection. Some researchers, such as Moss and Hendershot (2002) and Harkrader and Moore (1997), believe that male reluctant and remedial readers prefer to read nonfiction. Nonfiction material abounds on the Web in the form of electronic books and on Web sites. The United

States Geological Survey (USGS), for example, publishes a large number of short nonfiction e-books in HTML format at http://pubs.usgs.gov/products/books/gip.html (Figure 7.1). In the fiction genre, males tend to choose more science fiction, comedy, sports, war, and spy stories, while females generally choose more romances, horror/ghost, school, and poetry books (Pritchard, n.d.). For each of these preferences, libraries of free e-books are available. For example, Baen (www.baen.com) makes available on the Web more than 70 current science fiction books in multiple formats (Figure 7.2), and Harlequin (www.eharlequin.com/cms/index.jhtml) publishes romance serials weekly in HTML format on the eHarlequin Web site. Both publishing houses make books available at no cost to the reader.

Figure 7.1. The USGS Publications Warehouse offers several online publications.

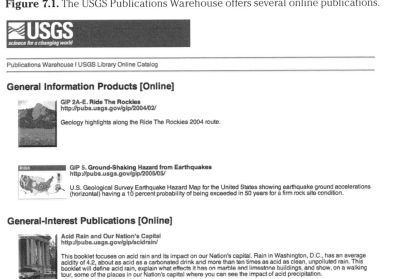

Figure 7.2. The Baen Free Library features science fiction books.

Incorporate Large-Print Materials

Students who struggle with reading, regardless of the reason, can benefit from changing to larger font sizes as a reading scaffold. While the use of large-print text has usually been associated with assisting the special needs of students with visual impairments or older people, the benefits gained with large print are actually applicable to students who may not have a learning disability, specifically the reluctant and remedial readers.

Students in all grades, especially those susceptible to visual stress, have been found to make more errors on the smaller rather than on the larger text. From this, Hughes and Wilkins (2000) concluded that the reading development of some children could benefit from a larger text size and spacing than is currently the norm. Reading miscues, including misreading syllables or words; skipping syllables, words, or lines; rereading lines; and ignoring punctuation cues were found to be virtually eliminated when students read large-print books. According to Elizabeth Lowe (2003), incorporating large-print text into reading programs for struggling readers has resulted in significant sustained improvement in word recognition and accuracy, comprehension, and fluency—the three forms of disabilities in reading.

Larger font sizes and spacing actually cause the eyes to move more slowly while reading, allowing students to track their reading more easily (Bloodsworth, 1993) and giving them more processing time. Fewer words on a page means struggling readers have less to visually process per page, but it still allows the student to make progress with comprehension, tracking, and fluency, with fewer decoding errors. Additionally, having fewer words on the page lowers anxiety levels concerning the text in struggling readers (Thorndike Press, 2004).

Font size, paper and ink colors, and formatting are all factors that affect the readability of text material (Fiske, 1994). Books in digital format can easily accommodate a change in typeface, text color, and background color.

Figure 7.3. Larger font sizes can make reading easier for struggling students.

COMPARISON OF FONT SIZES

newspaper classified ad
(8 point Times New Roman)

adult book
(11 point Times New Roman)

large-print book
(16 point Verdana)

Today's computers can produce a wide range of font sizes from 1 point to 1,638 points. The term *point* refers to the height of each letter. One inch is 72 points. Therefore, a point size of 18 equals one-quarter of an inch, and 36 points equals a half-inch. A size of 10 to 12 points is typical for adult books; a newspaper's classified ads are often printed in 8-point type. A good size for reluctant readers is 14 to 16 point type (Figure 7.3).

E-books are a great source for large-print books, with the added benefit that students can select the size of print they prefer. The size of e-book text can be changed either by enlarging the text or by "zooming" or magnifying the display. Notice the differences between the smallest versus the largest text display sizes with MS Reader in Figure 7.4.

Figure 7.4. A comparison of small text display and large text display.

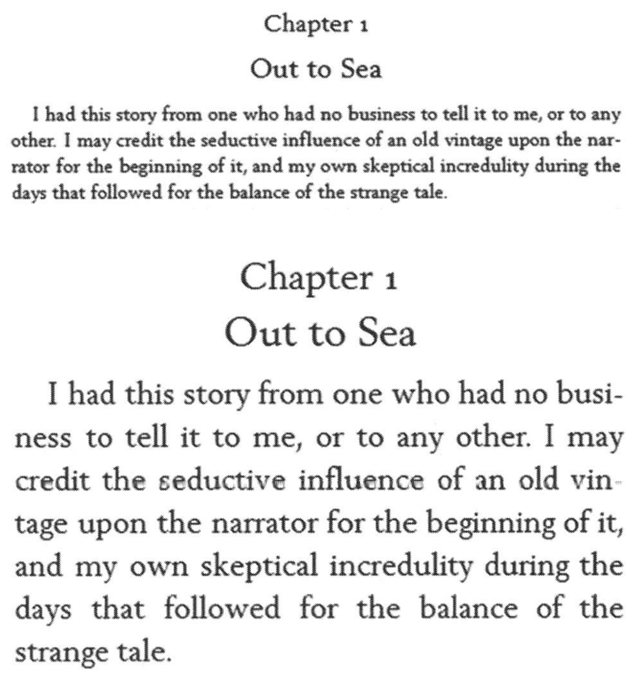

Chapter 1

Out to Sea

I had this story from one who had no business to tell it to me, or to any other. I may credit the seductive influence of an old vintage upon the narrator for the beginning of it, and my own skeptical incredulity during the days that followed for the balance of the strange tale.

Chapter 1

Out to Sea

I had this story from one who had no business to tell it to me, or to any other. I may credit the seductive influence of an old vintage upon the narrator for the beginning of it, and my own skeptical incredulity during the days that followed for the balance of the strange tale.

Engage Multiple Modalities

The Family Literacy Foundation (2002) states that studies show one of the most important things that can be done in preparing children for success in school and reading is to read aloud to them: reading aloud helps build listening, vocabulary, memory, and language skills and helps children learn information about the world around them. A reluctant or remedial reader may be troubled when reading a certain passage, but display good comprehension after listening to the same passage.

Kress (2003) in his book *Literacy in the New Media Age* advocates for a more multimodal approach to literacy instruction. This approach should include audio and image presentation, as today's students live in an age when text has evolved with new media forms, such as those displayed on computers and handheld computing devices.

E-book resources and applications that engage multiple modalities include text-to-speech programs, Web sites with multimedia Flash books, video through the Internet, and digital audio books. See chapter 6 for more information.

Teach Important Vocabulary

Vocabulary refers to the words we must know to communicate effectively, and it plays an important part in the reading process. Vocabulary is critical to reading comprehension; students can't understand what they're reading without understanding the meaning of the words. As students learn to read and progress, they must learn the meaning of new words.

The scientific research on vocabulary instruction reveals that:

- most of a student's vocabulary is learned indirectly when they hear and see words used in different contexts, and

- some vocabulary must be taught directly, as individual words and with word-learning strategies.

Direct vocabulary instruction aids reading comprehension. Students learn vocabulary best when they are provided with instruction over an extended period of time and when that instruction has them work actively with the words. Even though it can be difficult for students to master the use of dictionaries, glossaries, and thesauruses, learning to use them helps broaden and deepen their knowledge of words. Further, the most helpful dictionaries include sentences providing clear examples of word meanings in context (Armbruster, Lehr, & Osborn, 2003).

E-books provide a tremendous advantage in employing these resources. Many e-book formats allow immediate access to dictionaries and other reference works (Figure 7.5). When students come across an unfamiliar word, they simply click on the word and use an interactive dictionary to look up the definition. A student can also use the word search feature to find a word and see its contextual use. If the student uses the interactive dictionary to look up the definition of a word and the definition uses a word that the student doesn't understand, the interactive dictionary can look up that word instantly from within the definition. Many defined words are also hyperlinked to other definitions as "see" statements.

Using an interactive e-book dictionary, a student doesn't need to take the additional time and effort to leave his or her desk, get another book, riffle through the pages to find the definition, and then double check the word's context. Instead, the student merely clicks on the word for instant vocabulary assistance.

Figure 7.5. A word's definition is quickly accessed in MS Reader with its interactive dictionary.

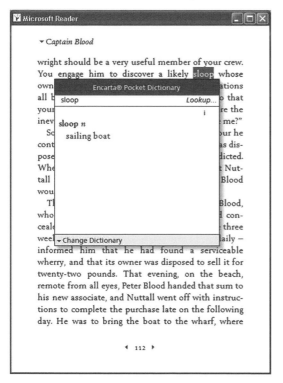

An Additional Strategy: Read the First Chapter

Kylee Beers (2003) suggests an additional strategy in assisting struggling readers, which is to read to the student the first chapter of a book. Her research indicates that reluctant readers are less reluctant if someone has read them the first chapter or two. A technology support that could assist with this strategy is the Random House book site (www.randomhouse.com), which sells a large number of audio books. The site provides excerpts of the first chapter or two in RealPlayer format for a number of these books. A student can listen to audio excerpts being read by a professional reader. Media specialist Nancy Keane uses book talks to get students interested in books, and has suggestions for more than 60 audio book excerpts that can be used with book talks (http://nancykeane.com/booktalks/audiobook.htm).

Conclusion

Students can be reluctant or remedial readers for a wide range or reasons—lack of motivation, materials being beyond their reading level, poor reading skills, low interest in the materials, inexperience with the English language, or even learning or print disabilities. Electronic books can be a tool to assist these readers. E-books can provide to the instructor and the student new options, scaffolds, and resources for reading materials at all levels and for all purposes.

Online Resources

Booksellers and Libraries

Baen Free Library (e-book library of modern science fiction): www.baen.com/library/

E-book Libraries (e-book libraries appropriate for education use): www.drscavanaugh. org/ebooks/ebook_libraries.htm#ChildrensLibraries

eHarlequin.com (romance fiction publishing house): www.eharlequin.com/cms/index. jhtml

United States Geological Survey (digital Earth science nonfiction library): http://pubs. usgs.gov/products/books/gip.html

Strategies

E-book Reading Strategies (reading strategies applied to digital text): www.drscavanaugh.org/e-books/ebrs/intro.htm

Nancy Keane's Book Talks Quick and Simple Site: http://nancykeane.com/booktalks/ Ms. Keane provides instructions for having a book talk, online resources, and links to audio excerpts from popular literature.

Put Reading First from the National Institute for Literacy: www.nifl.gov/nifl/publications. html

References

Allington, R. (2001). *What really matters for struggling readers: Designing research-based programs.* New York: Longman.

Allington, R. (2005, February). *What really matters for struggling readers?* Paper presented at the Wisconsin State Reading Association Convention, Milwaukee, WI. Retrieved June 2005 from http://www.uwex.edu/ics/stream/wsra/

Armbruster, B. B., Lehr, F., & Osborn, J. (2003). *Put reading first: The research building blocks for teaching children to read* (2nd ed.). Retrieved October 2004 from http://www.nifl.gov/ partnershipforreading/publications/PFRbooklet.pdf

Beers, K. (2003). *When kids can't read: What teachers can do: A guide for teachers 6–12.* Portsmouth, NH: Heinemann.

Beers, K., & Samuels, B. (1998). *Into focus: Understanding and creating middle school readers.* Norwood, MA: Christopher-Gordon.

Bloodsworth, J. G. (1993). *Legibility of print* (Report No. CS-011-244). East Lansing, MI: National Center for Research on Teacher Learning. (ERIC Document Reproduction Service No. ED355497.) Retrieved October 2004 from http://www.eric.ed.gov

Elley, W. B. (1992). *How in the world do students read? The IEA study of reading literacy.* The Hague, the Netherlands: International Association for the Evaluation of Educational Achievement.

Family Literacy Foundation. (2002). *Why read aloud with children?* Retrieved October 2004 from http://www.read2kids.org

Fiske, D. (1994). Removing obstacles to easy reading. *Technical Communication, (41)*2.

Harkrader, M. A., & Moore, R. (1997). Literature preferences of fourth graders. *Reading Research and Instruction, 36,* 325–339.

Hughes, L., & Wilkins, A. (2000). Typography in children's reading schemes may be suboptimal: Evidence from measures of reading rate. *Journal of Research in Reading, 23*(3), 314. Retrieved October 2004 from http://www.blackwellpublishing.com/journal.asp?ref=0141-0423

Krashen, S. (1995). School libraries, public libraries, and the NAEP reading scores. *School Library Media Quarterly, 23.*

Kress, G. (2003). *Literacy in the new media age.* London: Routledge.

Lowe, E. (2003, May). *Large print books: The missing link for speed and fluency for all students—struggling, proficient, in between.* Paper presented at the International Reading Association Conference, Orlando, FL.

Moss, B., & Hendershot, J. (2002). Exploring sixth graders' selection of nonfiction trade books. *The Reading Teacher, 56*(1), 6–17.

National Assessment of Education Progress (NAEP). (2001). *NAEP achievement levels for reading: 1992–1998.* Retrieved August 2005 from http://www.nagb.org/pubs/readingbook.pdf

National Center to Improve the Tools of Educators (NCITE). (1996). *Learning to Read/Reading to Learn Campaign: Helping children with learning disabilities to succeed.* Retrieved August 2005 from http://idea.uoregon.edu/~ncite/programs/read.html

Pritchard, L. (n.d.). *Understanding the reluctant male reader: Implications for the teacher librarian and the school library.* Retrieved October 2004 from http://www.penguin.com.au/PUFFIN/TEACHERS/Articles/understand_male.htm

Thorndike Press. (2004). *Large print and reading independence: Research summary and findings.* Retrieved October 2004 from http://www.galeschools.com/pdf/BenefitsofLargePrint.pdf

West-Christy, J. (2003). *Helping remedial and reluctant readers.* Retrieved October 2004 from http://www.glencoe.com/sec/teachingtoday/educationupclose.phtml/29

Chapter 8

E-books for Students with Special Needs

In today's teaching environment, all educators need to be prepared to make accommodations for students with special needs, such as disabilities or second language issues. Reading and writing are basic components of most educational activities, so providing alternative formats and supports becomes necessary to reach all students.

An accommodation is a change in the way that instruction is presented, but not a change in the content of the instruction, the skill being learned, or the material being assessed. Text provided in standard print format can create a barrier for students with dyslexia, visual impairments, and other disabilities. Several accommodations provided by digital text can be applied to break down that barrier.

How Digital Text Provides Accommodations

E-books have features that traditional paper books do not. Placing electronic files on small handheld devices enables students with physical impairments to carry a wealth of information. Simple changes in the text display can be an accommodation, such as enlarging the font or changing the contrast between the text and background. Another accommodation available with e-books is using text-to-speech software. Still others include annotations and concept maps, multi-language interactive dictionaries, and summarizing programs. Using the interactive features of modern e-books, instructors can create pre-accommodated or strategized e-books for student reading that include advance organizers, cooperative activities, and reading guides.

According to the Center for Applied Special Technology (CAST), to reach learners with disparate backgrounds, interests, styles, abilities, disabilities, and levels of expertise educational materials need to be flexible and adaptable for all learning styles (Rose & Meyer, 2000). Today's e-book and reader help meet those conditions.

Reduced Weight

With their current size, battery, memory, and display technology, handheld computers add a degree of mobility and access to text that was previously impossible. Many handhelds now run more than 10 hours on a charge, weigh less than two pounds, and carry several gigabytes of storage. The ability to carry books, reference material, and notes electronically allows any user to make better use of the information, but is a particular advantage for students with physical disabilities. Many physically impaired students are unable to carry the average 20-pound backpack (Petracco, 2001) filled with books, notes, and other resources. The amount of text in an e-book takes no additional space and adds no additional weight to the book, making handheld reader versions highly accessible to students with physical disabilities.

Furthermore, handhelds use a touch screen, allowing e-book navigation to be controlled with a single finger.

Adjustable Text Display

Standard printed text often presents barriers for students with dyslexia and visual impairments. E-book text is adaptable, allowing selection from a variety of sizes and font styles to meet the needs of each individual user (Figure 8.1). Larger text sizes can assist students who have vision impairments or motor disabilities that affect eye movement.

Figure 8.1. Font size and appearance can be adjusted to the most comfortable setting.

Techniques to improve readability include

- enlarging the font (Figure 8.1)
- blocking out part of the screen, which may be distracting
- adding highlighting
- changing the contrast between the text and background

See chapter 7 for more on changing the text display.

Many students with learning disabilities require assistive technology for help in reading. One example of assistive technology is the use of large-print materials, which improves visual processing by making the task of seeing the letters less difficult (Riviere, 1996). As the print is made larger, students view fewer words on the page, thus enabling them to focus more easily. The chance of students losing their place while reading is decreased.

According to galeschools.com (2004), many teachers and librarians already use large-print materials for their students who have:

- attention deficit disorder (ADD)
- difficulty with encoding or decoding
- dyslexia
- large or small motor deficits
- amblyopia or "lazy eye"
- light sensitivity
- short-term memory deficits
- tracking issues
- visual impairments

For more on large-print materials, see chapter 7.

The e-book program that I have found the most accommodating and advanced is MS Reader (www.microsoft.com/reader). MS Reader uses a text display format called ClearType, which causes text displayed on a screen to look like words in a printed book (Microsoft, 2001). While this e-book format may be the most accommodating available today for text display, other similarly friendly formats are sure to follow.

Text-to-Speech and Speech Synthesis

Some e-book formats will read text aloud on a desktop or laptop, and manufacturers are developing technology that allows handhelds to do the same.

Using a text-to-speech program offers users an additional modality for receiving information, and serves as an accommodation for various learning styles and individual differences in abilities (Gardner 1983; Theory into Practice Database, 2002).

A text-to-speech system is one that reads text aloud through the computer's sound card or other speech synthesis device. Text that is selected for reading is analyzed by the software, restructured to a phonetic system, and then read aloud. The computer evaluates each word, calculates its pronunciation (certain systems do this better than others), and then says the word in its context.

One student who I worked with who has dyslexia now uses text-to-speech software to improve his comprehension. He consistently uses the text-to-speech tool with technical reading, and has noticed not only increased comprehension, but also improved speed and retention. (See chapter 6 for more information on read-alouds.)

A component of many text-to-speech programs is synchronized highlighting of the text that is being read aloud. This speech with highlighting can aid students in recognizing the structure of written language. Text-to-speech with synchronized highlighting also assists students in learning proper scanning techniques as they follow the moving highlight from the top left and then progress across and down the page, go to the next page, and start-again. Students can also highlight words that they find difficult to decode, and then have the program say the word aloud. This spoken word support has been found to improve reading comprehension for students with reading difficulties (Wise & Olson, 1994). Some e-book programs already have text-to-speech built into them, while others, such as Adobe Reader and MS Reader, allow it to be added as a plug-in. Text-to-speech programs can also be purchased for reading text and Web pages, such as CAST's eReader (www.cast.org) and the IBM Home Page Reader (www-3.ibm.com/able/solution_offerings/hpr.html).

These systems are limited to a standard phonological structure, so foreign words, special personal pronunciations, or acronyms are often misspoken. Some text-to-speech systems will allow the user to adjust the pronunciation of words by changing their phonological "spelling" to the desired structure, which requires some knowledge of phonological structure by the user. Text-to-speech programs are now available in multiple languages, using the phonological structure of the target language.

Using electronic text and a text-to-speech program can have many advantages over plain printed text. A text-to-speech program or screen reader enables students with limited vision or reading disabilities to access the information they need. Research on students with reading disabilities found that comprehension improved when text-to-speech was combined with reading (Leong, 1995; Montali & Lewandowsi, 1996; Raskind & Shaw, 2000). Research findings suggest that student control of text-to-speech speed while they read along increases student performance. Some students benefit from a slower text-to-speech reading speed, while others comprehend better at faster rates (Shany & Biemiller, 1995; Skinner, Johnson, Larkin, Lessey, & Glowacki, 1995). Programs with text-to-speech usually have a control that governs the voice and rate of speech (Figure 8.2).

Figure 8.2. Microsoft Windows panel to control voice and speed of text-to-speech.

Studies have found advantages of using electronic text applications with struggling readers, in comparison with paper-based text (Reinking, Labbo, McKenna, & Kiefer, 1998). Anderson-Inman and Horney's (1999) studies indicated that students could access and use the scaffolding advantages of text-to-speech, online dictionaries, and note-taking offered through electronic text to achieve success in classroom assignments.

One new product is Thinking Reader, an e-book tool to assist students with special needs and struggling readers (www.tomsnyder.com/Products/Product.asp?SKU=THITHI). Developed by Tom Snyder Productions, Thinking Reader systematically builds reading comprehension skills by providing voice narration and synchronized highlighting. It embeds prompts, hints, model answers, and instant feedback into the text to provide individualized instruction. Thinking Reader also includes comprehensive support materials that make it easy for educators to integrate the program into a variety of instructional settings.

Teacher-Created Accommodations

Teachers can build accommodations into e-books they're creating to assist students with special needs, such as including extra blank pages, images, concept maps, notes, and even increased spacing between the words. Once an annotation file or dictionary has been created for the e-book on a computer, it can be distributed along with the book file so that special needs users will have the resource when they start reading their e-book. The files can be distributed as often as needed to as many users as desired. (See chapter 5 for more information on e-book reading strategies.)

Annotations and Concept Maps

A number of e-book programs allow the creation of annotations. Annotations include high-lights, bookmarks, notes, and drawings, all stored in one location where they can be easily viewed and organized. In MS Reader, annotations can be organized by type, page number, date created, or last modified (Figure 8.3).

Figure 8.3. Hyperlinks to all annotations through the Annotations table of contents.

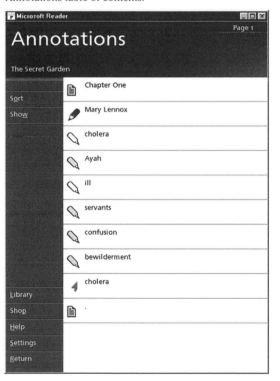

Using an annotation system, an educator can go through an e-book and prehighlight sections in multiple colors to assist readers. An educator can create and include advance organizers or notes to assist with the reading. Such notes may provide clues, hints, questions, or guides as accommodations. It's also possible to create and add concept maps as drawings to the annotations file.

Dictionaries

Interactive dictionaries allow users to select any word within the e-book and get a definition instantly. Some e-book programs offer foreign language dictionaries, which allow instant translation to a different language.

Free dictionary e-books can be downloaded to the computer for use by an e-book reader program. With this specialized e-book, the student can look up word meanings through a built-in "look up" function. For students with special needs, educators can create their own dictionaries with language adaptations, such as simpler language, context, or foreign languages. This custom dictionary can be selected as the current interactive dictionary.

The Summarize Feature

Another form of accommodation is to shorten the text or change it to a simpler form. One way to do this is to use a tool such as Word's AutoSummarize (see chapter 5). In Word, selecting **AutoSummarize** from the **Tools** menu brings up a window that lets a user determine how much of the text will be displayed in the summary.

A student with cognitive disability in one of my classes said he needed help reviewing books he was reading in his language arts class. While he had read the entire book from the class, he had trouble reviewing the material. I taught him how to create chapter summaries using the AutoSummarize tool, which enabled him to successfully review the material for a test. He was pleased that he was able to use this technique to work more effectively, while also making more efficient use of time with his tutor.

Changes in Wording

Another option is to change the actual wording of the text. An example is Mary Godolphin's conversion of three texts, *The Swiss Family Robinson, Robinson Crusoe*, and *The Pilgrim's Progress*. Godolphin changed multisyllable words to single-syllable words, except personal names. Where this wasn't possible, she wrote out the word in all capital letters and broke up the word by syllable, for example, SUG-AR CANE (Figure 8.4). All of these books are available for download from the Blackmask Online library. I recommended the *Robinson Crusoe* single-syllable book recently to an ESOL student, and she was very excited to find a book in English that she could understand that was also being read by her schoolmates.

Figure 8.4. At left is *The Swiss Family Robinson* original work, by Johann Wyss. At right is the same text in words of one syllable, converted by Mary Godolphin.

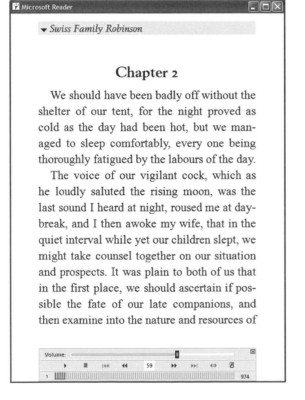
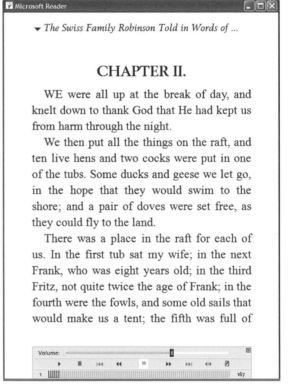

A Real-Life Example

To exemplify how it is possible to make a book more accommodating, I'll describe a recent project to adapt a book for a special needs situation, *The Secret Garden*, by Francis Hodgson Burnett. The book is often used as a multidisciplinary tool for teaching language, science, and health.

In adapting this book, I first faced the question of whether I wanted to create the e-book file or use files that already existed. As the book is in the public domain and therefore copyright free, I found numerous copies available in the e-book format that I wanted. One was from Blackmask Online (www.blackmask.com), which distributes e-books in multiple formats including the MS Reader format that I desired.

While all the copies of *The Secret Garden* e-books I found were good, they didn't contain all the features that I wanted to include. I decided to create my own e-book by downloading a text-only version and opening it into a Web page editor. I then added some HTML code that would allow me to insert page breaks and to create a blank page before the start of each chapter. I also decided to create a new e-book file because I wished to add some additional sections and components. In several chapters I added copyright free public domain pictures from a variety of sources to serve as associated images for the chapter, and I created concept maps for the characters and storyline. I also created a reader guide and story outline file that would be associated with but not inserted into the text of the book.

Then I used the ReaderWorks (www.overdrive.com) program to create the e-book LIT file (see chapter 10 for more on creating e-books). This process also creates a "clickable" table of contents to each chapter, image, and associated file. Using this table of contents, a student can quickly jump to any chapter or call up in a pop-up window the associated reader guide, outline, or any of the concept maps that had been created.

With the book now in the MS Reader e-book format, I developed additional accommodations. For each chapter I highlighted passages or components that were important or that a student with special needs might have difficulty with. These sections were highlighted in different colors to provide additional direction. Then I added an advance-reading organizer for students to read before starting each chapter, and a set of summary questions at the end of each chapter (Figure 8.5). These questions were added to the book as annotations and are indicated on the page with a nonintrusive mark that can be clicked to access the content. Students can also add their own notes, questions, and answers to the text box.

I added bookmarks for passages that related to specific topics, such as science. While

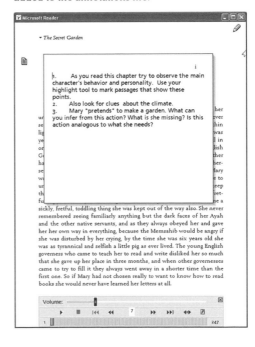

Figure 8.5. Guided reading questions have been added to the annotations file.

Figure 8.6. An accommodating electronic textbook from Holt, Rinehart, and Winston provides interactive tools and reading help.

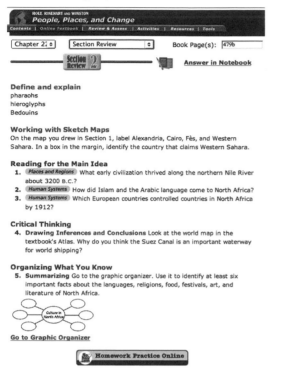

reading the book, students can also add their own bookmarks to indicate pages that they wish to return to or will need assistance with. This collection of annotations, both the ones that I created and the ones that students create as they read, becomes an associated file that can be accessed through an Annotations table of contents. To give the student the associated annotations, all that is needed is to place the e-book file (LIT file) and the annotation file (EBO file) on the student's computer hard drive in the **My Library** and **Annotations** folders within the **My Documents** folder. This process allows me to keep the master e-book files while the students have their own individual files.

Obtaining E-books for Students with Special Needs

Textbooks

If an educator is using a standard textbook with a class and needs to obtain an electronic version for a student with special needs, digital versions can be requested from the publishers. Usually this is accomplished though the office of student services or the school district special education department. The request process can take awhile and often requires special forms and permissions concerning copyright. One student I taught who was legally blind needed her books in an electronic format so that she could use her text-to-speech tool to "read" the course materials. While the process of requesting the electronic text version from the textbook publisher took some time and work on my part, once the material was received, my student was able to successfully keep up with the class.

Educators should check to see whether an electronic version of the textbook is already available, as many school book publishers publish Web-based versions of their textbooks (see chapter 4 for more on electronic textbooks). With a text-format electronic textbook, students should be able to change the size of the text, use screen magnification software, integrate a text-to-speech program, use translating software, or print to Braille.

Recordings for the Blind & Dyslexic (www.rfbd.org) is the number one producer in the world of audio textbooks for people who can't effectively read standard print. It offers audio books recorded in specialized formats, such as four-track cassettes or digitally recorded books on CD. Its CD books offer quick and easy navigation by page, chapter, or section.

Some publishers have added support features with digital textbooks. For example, Holt, Rinehart, and Winston (www.hrw.com) books have reader tools that includes highlighting, annotations, bookmarks, help files (Figure 8.6), and a special reading comprehension tool called Live Ink. Live Ink provides reading support through visual cues of color and position of the text's content.

Trade Books

For trade books, search the free online libraries for existing copies. E-books can be easily converted to other formats for use in text-to-speech software. See chapter 6 for more on converting text to speech.

One option for obtaining trade books is for an individual or school to contract with a special needs book subscription service such as the Accessible Book Collection in HTML format (www.accessible-bookcollection.org). Subscriptions are discussed in the next section.

Bookshare.org (www.bookshare.org) has more than 17,000 e-books in its collection, including many on the Accelerated Reader list, and it makes them available in multiple formats of basic text, Web, MP3 audio, and DAISY (see box).

Special Needs Subscriptions

Companies such as Bookshare.org (www.bookshare.org) and the Accessible Book Collection (www.accessiblebookcollection.org) provide an important service to schools and students by offering digital text to qualified persons with special needs, such as low vision, blindness, reading disabilities, dyslexia, and mobility impairments. Usually subscribers need to be certified or sponsored by either a physical or educational specialist, which could be a teacher or librarian. The average cost is $50–$100 annually.

DAISY
(Digital Accessible Information System)

DAISY is a standard for producing books in an electronic format accessible for print-impaired readers. Books produced using the DAISY standard offer people with learning disabilities a multisensory approach to reading. They can listen to a book while reviewing the text in print, and navigate through the audio or electronic text version by moving among the headings, chapters, and pages. Books may be accessed with a portable player or by computer. If text is included, some software allows users to have the text on the computer screen highlighted as it is read aloud. For more information about DAISY, visit www.daisy.org.

BRF
(Braille Ready File)

The BRF format is a digital Braille format. BRFs are preformatted for pages 25 lines deep and 40 cells wide and may be read with a refreshable Braille display, printed on a Braille embosser, or translated by a computer using a text-to-speech system or device.

Different organizations provide their e-books as accessible materials in different ways. For example, the Accessible Book Collection makes books in a large Web format with additional controls for background color. The e-books can also be used with a text-to-speech program for audio output.

The Bookshare.org makes its materials available to users in BRF, DAISY, HTML, and text formats, which can be used with a browser to vary the text size or with a text-to-speech program (see box for descriptions of BRF and DAISY). Bookshare.org also makes its more than 17,000 e-books available as machine read audio files in MP3 format.

Most organizations will cross-reference their collection with other school applications such as Accelerated Reader.

Figure 8.7. The News-2-You weekly paper provides words with picture support.

News-2-You

Another type of subscription service found to be effective with special needs, second language, and emergent readers is a weekly news service called News-2-You (www.news-2-you.com). News-2-You is a newspaper, delivered through the Internet, that provides reading support with symbols (see Figure 8.7 for a sample page).

Teachers who use News-2-You in their classrooms have found that the weekly paper engages students with high-interest topics.

With a subscription, a school or educator receives 38 issues a year in Adobe PDF format. Each publication has a regular edition, a simplified edition, a higher edition, and a communication board with vocabulary words (see box). Subscribers receive 25–30 pages per issue, including 8–12 pages about a current event. All pages relate to the weekly lead story. Additional newspaper pages can be accessed online covering topics such as weather, sports, birthday news, movie and book reviews, and localized news.

Communication Board

A communication board is an augmentative communication chart that people without speech or with difficulty with certain words can use to communicate. The visual representation may include photographs, picture communication symbols, Bliss symbols, alphabet letters, words, or other means of communication. On the simplest communication boards, a student points at a symbol to communicate, while electronic boards speak aloud when a symbol is pressed. Some connect to a computer and serve as both an input and communication device (Figure 8.8). Contact your special education department for more information on communication boards.

Figure 8.8. A News-2-You communication board is being used as an Intellikeys overlay.

Copyright Exemption

Usually it would be a violation of copyright to share or distribute copyrighted works of literature as these organizations do. An exception in the U.S. copyright law makes these distributions possible as long as the copyrighted books are available only to people with real disabilities. The exception in Section 17 U.S.C. § 121 of the copyright law states in part:

> It is not an infringement of copyright for an authorized entity to reproduce or to distribute copies or phonorecords of a previously published, nondramatic literary work if such copies or phonorecords are reproduced or distributed in specialized formats exclusively for use by blind or other persons with disabilities. (U.S. Code, 2000)

This exemption makes it possible for authorized nonprofit organizations and governmental agencies to convert copyrighted materials to formats such as Braille, audio, or digital text for use by people with disabilities.

Conclusion

With today's e-book technologies, educators have valuable tools for assisting learners with diverse abilities, language backgrounds, and reading levels. These unique features include variable text size, text-to-speech, and interactions that many students need to be successful readers. Now that it is easier than ever to obtain electronic texts, educators need to seriously consider using e-books to provide accommodations for students with special needs. Help for these students may be literally at your fingertips.

Online Resources

Library

Blackmask (free digital library): www.blackmask.com

Reading Support

Holt, Rinehart, and Winston: www.hrw.com
The textbook publisher offers digital textbooks with accommodations.

Intersect Digital Library: http://intersect.uoregon.edu/default.html
This collection of HTML formatted books includes reading support strategies and tools designed to help students learn more from what they read.

News-2-You (weekly digital newspaper with picture/symbol support): www.news-2-you.com

The Secret Garden: www.drscavanaugh.org/ebooks/samples_and_applications.htm
Scroll down the page to find links to accommodated book examples for download.

Services

Accessible Book Collection: www.accessiblebookcollection.org
The collection offers an e-book subscription service for readers with special needs.

Bookshare.org: www.bookshare.org
This e-book subscription service is geared toward readers with special needs.

Recordings for the Blind & Dyslexic: www.rfbd.org
This audio book subscription service is geared toward readers with special needs.

Software

Adobe Reader: www.adobe.com

CAST's eReader (Web browser with text-to-speech): www.cast.org

IBM Home Page Reader (Web browser with text-to-speech): www-3.ibm.com/able/solution_offerings/hpr.html

MS Reader: www.microsoft.com/reader

Thinking Reader: www.tomsnyder.com/Products/Product.asp?SKU=THITHI
This e-book reader provides reading strategies and comprehension support.

References

Anderson-Inman, L., & Horney, M. (1999). *Electronic books: Reading and studying with supportive resources.* Retrieved July 2004 from http://www.readingonline.org/electronic/ebook/index.html

galeschools.com. (2004). *Thorndike Press Struggling Reader Center.* Retrieved October 2004 from http://www.galeschools.com/thorndike/index.htm

Gardner, H. (1983). *Frames of mind: The theory of multiple intelligences.* New York: Basic Books.

Leong, C. K. (1995). Effects of on-line reading and simultaneous DECtalk auditing in helping below-average and poor readers comprehend and summarize text. *Learning Disability Quarterly, 18*(2), 101–117.

Microsoft. (2001). *ClearType Information.* Retrieved August 2005 from http://www.microsoft.com/typography/ClearTypeInfo.mspx

Montali, J., & Lewandowski, L. (1996). Bimodal reading: Benefits of a talking computer for average and less skilled readers. *Journal of Learning Disabilities, 29*(3), 271–279.

Petracco, P. (2001, May/June). Weighing in on backpacks. *School Leader.* Retrieved November 2004 from http://www.njsba.org/members_only/publications/school_leader/May-June-2001/info_link.htm

Reinking, D., Labbo, L., McKenna, M., & Kiefer, R. (Eds.). (1998). *Handbook of literacy and technology.* Hillsdale, NJ: Erlbaum.

Riviere, A. (1996). *Assistive technology: Meeting the needs of adults with learning disabilities* (Report No. EC-305-177). East Lansing, MI: National Center for Research on Teacher Learning. (ERIC Document Reproduction Service No. ED401686.) Retrieved October 2004 from http://www.eric.ed.gov

Rose, D., & Meyer, A. (2000). *The future is in the margins: The role of technology and disability in educational reform.* Washington, DC: U.S. Department of Education, Office of Educational Technology. Retrieved July 2004 from http://www.cast.org/udl/index.cfm?i=542

Shany, M. T., & Biemiller, A. (1995). Assisted reading practice: Effects on performance of poor readers in grades 3 and 4. *Reading Research Quarterly, 30*(3), 382–395.

Skinner, C. H., Johnson, C. W., Larkin, M. J., Lessey, D. J., & Glowacki, M. L. (1995). The influence of rate of presentation during taped word interventions on reading performance. *Journal of Emotional and Behavioral Disorders, 3*(4), 214–223.

Theory into Practice Database. (2002). *Multiple intelligences.* Retrieved July 2004 from http://tip.psychology.org/

U.S. Code. (2000). *Copyright law of the United States of America and related laws contained in Title 17.* Retrieved November 2004 from www.copyright.gov/title17/92chap1.html

Wise, B. W., & Olson, R. K. (1994). Computer speech and the remediation of reading and spelling problems. *Journal of Special Education Technology, 12*(3), 207–220.

E-book Sources

Expanding Your E-book Collection

How large is your classroom book budget? If yours is like mine, it hasn't increased lately, so I often depend on free online libraries for additional resources.

The International Reading Association (IRA) states that school and classroom libraries should have adequate amounts of reading material for each student. For a classroom library, an adequate amount means approximately seven books of quality literature per student. A school library should have a minimum of 20 books per student. At least one new book per classroom and two per school library should be added for each student every year (IRA, 1999).

If you're having trouble finding funds for that many books, consider dipping into the well of free online libraries. You'll find public domain texts encompassing much of classic literature, science, and philosophy. Many online libraries provide electronic books, documents, articles, newspapers, and other forms of text. Free public libraries, such as the Internet Public Library (www.ipl.org), Project Gutenberg (www.promo.net/pg/), Blackmask Online (www.blackmask.com), and the University of Virginia Library (http://etext.lib.virginia.edu/), provide general and specialized works of public domain materials. According to Project Gutenberg (2001), in the year 2000 more than 20,000 free e-books were available online. That number grows daily.

If money isn't so tight, you can also purchase e-books at many locations, both online and off. Major booksellers, such as Amazon.com (www.amazon.com), sell current bestsellers often at prices lower than printed material. For example, when Carl Hiaasen's *Flush* was first released in 2005, the print version had a list price of $16.95, while Amazon.com offered the digital version for sale, in either Adobe or MS Reader format, for only $4.99.

Another option is for you or your students to create your own e-books. Not only does this allow you to choose the material you want for an e-book, it also gives students an opportunity to work closely with technology.

Once you feel comfortable locating or creating your own e-books, you can expand your collection further by subscribing to or building an e-book library. The next three chapters delve deeply into these topics, examining ways to locate e-books, create e-books, and build an entire digital library.

References

International Reading Association (IRA). (1999). *Providing books and other print materials for classroom and school libraries: A position statement.* Newark, DE: Author.

Project Gutenberg. (2001). *Project Gutenberg official home site.* Retrieved January 2005 from http://www.promo.net/pg/

Chapter 9

Finding E-books

This chapter focuses on ways teachers can find e-books that fit their curricular needs. With thousands of e-books available from bookstores and digital libraries, teachers have access to book resources like never before. The first part of this chapter provides an overview of e-book stores and libraries, and the middle portion is divided into specific categories of online library, such as those devoted to the elementary classroom or special collections. The chapter ends with search tools and techniques for evaluating the reading difficulty of the e-books you acquire.

E-book Bookstores

E-books are sold in a variety of formats and through a variety of methods. E-book references can be purchased on CD from office supply stores. Most local bookstores stock audio books, and many toy stores stock children's CD storybooks and e-books for special reading devices such as LeapPad and PowerTouch. The main method of purchasing e-book files for reading with a computer or other handheld device, however, is through Internet bookstores.

Many current bestsellers are available from online bookstores for purchase and download. Audio books from Audible (www.audible.com) include recent fiction and nonfiction, as well as radio shows and audio versions of newspapers and magazines. Online bookstores such as Amazon (www.amazon.com) and Contentlink (www.contentlinkinc.com) sell not only hard cover and paperback books but audio books and e-books for the Adobe Reader, MS Reader, and eReader programs.

When purchasing a book it might be important to consider its DRM (Digital Rights Management) level. The DRM level explains the extent to which the e-book is "locked." An e-book with a DRM at level 2 means that the book can be read on any device, with the right software, but not edited or changed. An e-book with a DRM level of 5, the highest level, is an owner exclusive e-book and can be read only on specific devices for which the owner is registered. Often text-to-speech software can't be used on an e-book with a level 5 restriction. Table 8 details the DRM levels, which have been developed into levels 2, 3, and 5.

Following is a list of online audio and text-format e-book stores.

Table 8. Digital Rights Management Levels

DRM LEVEL	DRM NAME	RESTRICTIONS	CLASSROOM IMPLICATION
❷	Sealed	■ Text cannot be changed. ■ E-book can be read with any copy of the reader software.	Technically the book file can be copied, but copyright restrictions do apply.
❸	Inscribed	■ Text cannot be changed. ■ E-book can be read with any copy of the reader software. ■ Owner's name is displayed.	
❺	Owner Exclusive	■ Text cannot be changed. ■ E-book can be read only with the reader software that has been activated and logged in by the owner.	E-book cannot be given away or placed on multiple machines without a specific owner logging in (and there is a limit to the number of machines on which the e-book may be loaded).

Audio E-book Stores

Audible: www.audible.com

Audio Books for Free: www.audiobooksforfree.com

Brilliance Audio: www.brillianceaudio.com

Recorded Books: www.recordedbooks.com

Text-Format E-book Stores

Amazon: www.amazon.com

Baen Science Fiction—WebScriptions: www.baen.com

Contentlink: www.contentlinkinc.com

CyberRead: http://cyberread.com/

Diesel eBooks: www.diesel-ebooks.com

eBookMall: www.ebookmall.com

eReader.com: www.ereader.com

Fictionwise: www.fictionwise.com

Powells.com: www.powells.com

Free Online Libraries

Educators should check before purchasing an e-book to see if that book is available for free elsewhere. A large number of classic books, pre-1920s, have passed into the public domain and are available for download from one of the free online libraries. Online libraries include the Internet Public Library (www.ipl.org), Florida Electronic Library (www.flelibrary.org), Blackmask Online (www.blackmask.com), and Project Gutenberg (www.gutenberg.org), which is the oldest of the online book repositories. Gutenberg has more than 10,000 copyright-free publications, from the library's first e-book, *Alice in Wonderland*, to the *Human Genome Project*. The University of Virginia Library (http://etext.lib.virginia.edu/) claims to have more than 50,000 electronic texts, distributing on average 9,000 e-books per day. Some of the online libraries store and distribute books in multiple formats, and some have special collections aimed at specific languages, content areas, or age groups.

As of 2004, the Million Book Project had digitized more than 80,000 free e-books. There are literally thousands of e-books available online for free along with thousands more for sale. Sometimes finding appropriate and useful texts can be difficult, but an analysis that I did comparing online resource libraries with reading lists for several states shows that many books required for the classroom are housed online in digital format and available for free.

Elementary E-book Resources

The following digital library and resource sites provide e-books that meet many of the needs of elementary classrooms. Sites such as the Internet Public Library KidSpace (Figure 9.1) host picture books, read-aloud books, short stories, and chapter books. While most of the sites have e-books designed to be downloaded or read online, some have books that can be printed. In some cases the reading materials are already leveled, such as at Reading A–Z and childrenselibrary.com. These resources provide students with access to a wide range of books at all levels.

NOTE: The icon indicates that the library has an audio version or support.

Aesop's Fables: www.umass.edu/aesop/contents.html
Fables in traditional and modern forms, most in HTML with some in Flash.

 Amazing Adventure Series: www.amazingadventure.com
Children's stories that can be read on the screen or read aloud in Flash format.

arts-entertainment-recreation.com: www.arts-entertainment-recreation.com/Arts/Literature/Children's_Literature/Online_Books/
Links to a variety of online children's books.

BAB Books: www.sundhagen.com/babbooks/
More than 12 online HTML picture books.

BookPALS (Performing Artists for Literacy in Schools): www.bookpals.net/storyline/
Stories read by members of the Screen Actors Guild (and others). Stories are read and displayed in a video screen (Windows Media, Real, and QuickTime). An additional story is available by phone from www.bookpals.net/storyline/phone.html.

Book-Pop: www.bookpop.com/bookpop.html
HTML picture books with the option to have the book read aloud.

byGosh.com: www.bygosh.com
Children's classics in HTML format.

 Candlelight Stories: www.candlelightstories.com/HelpOFoodMem.htm
Children's and chapter books in a variety of formats.

Children's Books Online, the Rosetta Project (formerly Editec Communications'
Children's Books for Free Library): www.childrensbooksonline.org
Site hosts 1,200 HTML children's books first published in the 19th and early 20th
centuries.

childrensclibrary.com: www.childrenselibrary.com
An online bookstore for teachers and schools, this company offers a 30-day trial
program to allow teachers to download and use e-books with their classes (LIT).

Children's Storybooks Online: www.magickeys.com/books/
Illustrated children's stories in HTML.

Class Conscious Big Books: www.classconsciousbooks.com/bigbooks.html
Young children's stories, HTML format.

 Clifford's Interactive Storybooks: http://teacher.scholastic.com/clifford1/
Interactive stories about Clifford the Big Red Dog in Flash format, presented by
Scholastic.

E-book Libraries: www.drscavanaugh.org/ebooks/ebook_libraries.
htm#ChildrensLibraries
A master list with links of online libraries useful for educators, including children's
books.

Florida Electronic Library: www.flelibrary.org
Public online library with magazines, newspapers, books, documents, and more
(HTML and PDF).

International Children's Digital Library (ICDL): www.icdlbooks.org
The ICDL is building an international collection that reflects both the diversity and
quality of children's literature from 27 cultures in 23 languages (HTML).

Internet Public Library KidSpace: www.ipl.org/div/kidspace/
This section of IPL contains The Reading Zone, which is similar to the fiction section
at a public library. There are links to online stories and links to information about
favorite books and authors.

 Mighty Book Catalogue: www.mightybook.com/catalogue.htm
More than 50 children's books for ages 2 through preteen in HTML. Books will read
aloud.

 NASA Books

- Online stories *Echo the Bat* and *Amelia the Pigeon* (HTML): http://imagers.gsfc.
nasa.gov/

- *Robin Whirlybird on her Rotorcraft Adventures* (HTML): http://rotored.arc.nasa.gov
A story and activities about a girl visiting her mother's work in English, Spanish,
and Chinese.

■ *Our Very Own Star* and *Auroras!* (Flash format): http://stargazer.gsfc.nasa.gov/epo/jsp/products.jsp

Reader's Theater Editions: www.aaronshep.com/rt/RTE.html
A collection of free scripts for reader's theater, adapted from stories by Aaron Shepard and others.

Reader's Theater Scripts and Plays: www.teachingheart.net/readerstheater.htm
Links to more than 50 reader's theater scripts on the Web.

Reading A–Z: www.readinga-z.com
An online bookseller of leveled books to print. Sample books are available (PDF).

RIF Reading Planet: www.rif.org/readingplanet/content/read_aloud_stories.mspx
A collection of read-aloud books that changes monthly (Flash format).

Sebastian Swan's Infant Explorer: www.naturegrid.org.uk/infant/
Eight big books in HTML.

Stories from Indonesia: www.geocities.com/kesumawijaya/
Seven HTML text stories.

StoryPlace: www.storyplace.org
More than 20 stories for elementary children along with suggested readings and print out activities.

Tales of Wonder: www.darsie.net/talesofwonder/index.html
Folk and fairy tales from around the world in HTML.

United States of America's Korean War Commemoration: http://korea50.army.mil/teachers/index.shtml
Two online picture books (HTML).

Figure 9.1. The Internet Public Library provides a children's section named KidSpace.

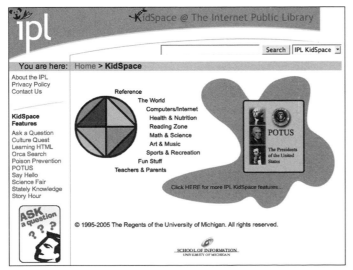

Figure 9.2. The Classic Book Library hosts more than 125 free e-books of classic material.

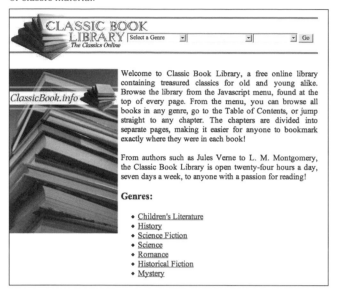

Secondary and General E-book Resources

Educators will find a wide range of secondary and general e-book resources online, including references, modern publications, and public domain books, many of which are considered classics. The Classic Book Library, for instance, hosts more than 125 free e-books of classic material (Figure 9.2). As a general rule, almost everything published in the United States since 1923 is subject to copyright restrictions, while nearly everything published before 1923 is in the public domain. In addition to public domain books, some libraries, such as Bartleby.com (Figure 9.3) and the Baen Free Library, make available a large number of copyrighted books as part of their free online collections.

NOTE: The icon 🎧 indicates that the library has an audio version or support.

Abacci Books: www.abacci.com/books/default.asp
Digital text versions of classic literature with reviews from Amazon (TXT and LIT).

Alex Catalog of Electronic Texts: http://sunsite.berkeley.edu/alex or www.infomotions.com/alex/
A catalog with roughly 2,000 links to e-texts, located on various servers.

American Library Association: www.ala.org/parentspage/greatsites/lit.html
More than 700 sites for children covering literature and language.

Aportis Library: www.aportis.com/library/index.html
More than 5,000 "AportisDoc" or DOC format files.

Audio Books for Free: www.audiobooksforfree.com
More than 300 audio books (as MP3 files) available for free download.

Baen Free Library: www.baen.com/library/
More than 50 recent science fiction books in MS Reader, eReader, Rocket, and RTF formats.

Bartleby.com: www.bartleby.com
Classic books and references in HTML.

Bibliomania: www.bibliomania.com
More than 2,000 texts of classic literature, book notes, references, and resources in HTML.

Blackmask Online: www. blackmask.com
More than 10,000 texts in a variety of formats, including LIT, HTML, and PDS.

BookRags: www.bookrags.com
Book notes and more than 1,500 novels (HTML).

Books2GoLibrary.com: www. books2golibrary.com/e-books_ free.html
E-books for eReader, Pocket PC, and desktop PC.

CIA Publication Library: www.cia. gov/cia/publications/index.html
Hosts the World Factbook with information on every country in the world.

Classic Book Library: http:// classicbook.info/index.html
More than 125 books in seven genres done in HTML page-by-page format.

Digital Text Project: www.ilt. columbia.edu/publications/ digitext.html
Links to works by famous philosophers.

DotLit: www.dotlit.com
Hosts only LIT files for MS Reader.

Electronic Text Center at the University of Virginia Library: http://etext.lib. virginia.edu/
Thousands of XML, HTML, MS Reader, and eReader texts.

Elegant Solutions Software Company: http://esspc-ebooks.com/default.htm
MS Reader books in a variety of genres.

The English Server's Fiction Collection: http://eserver.org/fiction/
Works of and about fiction.

Florida Electronic Library: www.flelibrary.org
Public online library with magazines, newspapers, books, documents, and more (HTML and PDF).

The Franklin Free Library: www.franklin.com/freelibrary/
More than 1,000 TXT and HTML files.

 FreE-books.org: www.freebooks.org
Lots of books in both TXT and MP3 formats.

Figure 9.3. Bartleby.com provides classics and reference books.

Internet Public Library: www.ipl.org/div/books
Links to more than 40,000 titles.

LiteralSystems.org: http://literalsystems.org/files/
More than 45 audio e-books of classic literature and poetry.

Litrix Reading Room: www.litrix.com/readroom.htm
More than 300 public domain titles in HTML chapter format.

Making of America: http://cdl.library.cornell.edu/moa/
Cornell University Library created this digital library of primary sources in American social history (antebellum through reconstruction periods). This is a full text/image journal site of 22 magazines from the 1830s to the 1900s.

manybooks.net: http://manybooks.net/
More than 10,000 eReader, Pocket PC, Zaurus, Rocket, and PDA e-books.

National Academies Press: www.nap.edu
Search and read the full text of this publisher's digitized books on various topics.

On-Line Books: http://onlinebooks.library.upenn.edu/
More than 15,000 listings, most in TXT format.

Page-by-Page Books: www.pagebypagebooks.com
More than 400 books to be read online (HTML).

PocketRocketFX.com: www.pocketrocketfx.com/html/ebooks.htm
Classics library in MS Reader format.

Project Gutenberg: http://promo.net/pg/
Oldest online library, E-books are usually TXT only, but some are offered in multiple formats including audio.

Read Print: www.readprint.com
Thousands of books for students, teachers, and the classic enthusiast in HTML.

WebBooks.com: www.Web-books.com/default.htm
More than 1,000 classic texts usually in MS Reader format.

Wired for Books: www.wiredforbooks.org
Collections of audio books and interviews. Contains full versions of *A Christmas Carol*, *Alice in Wonderland*, and Beatrix Potter stories along with short stories and excerpts from other books (RealPlayer).

World eBook Library: http://netlibrary.net/WorldHome.html
More than 27,000 free e-books in HTML format.

Special Collections

The online public domain libraries can provide teachers and students with access to books that would otherwise be unavailable. A number of online libraries now house and distribute works that are no longer in print, and some have special collections, such as the African American collection by and about African Americans at the University of Virginia Library and the censorship collection at Banned Books Online, hosted by the University of Pennsylvania Library (Figure 9.4).

Figure 9.4. Banned Books Online is a special collection of e-books that have been censored in the past.

The Online Books Page

presents

BANNED BOOKS ONLINE

Welcome to this special exhibit of books that have been the objects of censorship or censorship attempts. The books featured here, ranging from *Ulysses* to *Little Red Riding Hood*, have been selected from the indexes of The Online Books Page. (See that page for over 20,000 more online books!)

This page is a work in progress, and more works may be added to this page over time. Please inform **onlinebooks@pobox.upenn.edu** of any new material that can be included here. Note that the listings are meant to be representative rather than exhaustive. Also, many recent books that have been banned or challenged have not been included here, because they have not been made available online. (But see below).

Books Suppressed or Censored by Legal Authorities

Ulysses by James Joyce was selected by the Modern Library as the best novel of the 20th century, and has received wide praise from other literature scholars, including those who have defended online censorship. (Carnegie Mellon English professor and vice-provost Erwin Steinberg, who praised the book in 1994, also defended CMU's declaration that year to delete alt.sex and some 80 other newsgroups, claiming they were legally obligated to do so.) *Ulysses* was barred from the United States as obscene for 15 years, and was seized by U.S Postal Authorities in 1918 and 1930. The lifting of the ban in 1933 came only after advocates fought for the right to publish the book.

© 2005 by John Mark Ockerbloom. Used by permission.

E-book Collections
(Also see the content area e-book lists in chapter 4.)

African American: http://etext.lib.virginia.edu/subjects/African-American.html
E-books by and about African Americans.

Andamooka: www.andamooka.org/reader.pl
Technology and computer e-books.

Banned Books Online: http://onlinebooks.library.upenn.edu/banned-books.html
An exhibit of books that have been subjected to censorship or censorship attempts.

Christmas Stories: www.ucalgary.ca~dkbrown/christmas.html
More than 25 stories of Christmas.

Figure 9.5. BookRags is an online literature resource with study guides.

Digital Math Archive: http://sunsite.ubc.ca/DigitalMathArchive/
Collection of mathematical sources, focusing on documents from the late 19ᵗʰ century through the present.

E-Asia digital library: http://e-asia.uoregon.edu
More than 1,000 e-books on China, Japan, Korea, and Taiwan.

Florida Heritage Collection: http://susdl.fcla.edu/fh/
Materials representing Florida's history, culture, art, literature, and science.

Library of Southern Literature: http://docsouth.unc.edu/southlit/
Wide range of literary works from the American South published before 1924.

Native American: http://etext.lib.virginia.edu/subjects/Native-American.html
E-books by and about Native Americans.

Victorian Women Writers Project: www.indiana.edu/~letrs/vwwp/
Transcriptions of works by British women writers of the 19th century.

Women Writers: http://etext.lib.virginia.edu/subjects/Women-Writers.html
E-books by women writers.

Book Notes and Study Guides

BookRags: www.bookrags.com
Book notes and more than 1,500 novels in HTML (Figure 9.5).

Owleyes: www.owleyes.org
Offers help with understanding and writing about 12 famous literary works.

SparkNotes: www.sparknotes.com
SparkNotes (like Cliff Notes) offers help in understanding literature.

Other E-books

Artbomb.net: www.artbomb.net/comics.jsp#
Hosts five graphic novels.

Comics.com: www.unitedmedia.com/categories/index.html
More than 88 newspaper comic strips archived for the last 30 days.

King Features: www.kingfeatures.com/features/comics/comics.htm
More than 60 newspaper comic strips with a 30-day archive.

Newspapers on the Internet: www.ims.uni-stuttgart.de/info/Newspapers.html
Listing of newspapers from around the world that can be read online.

Slate: http://slate.msn.com/
An online magazine that is also published as an e-book.

UComics.com: www.ucomics.com/comics/
More than 60 daily newspaper comic strips.

Teacher E-books

Some libraries and e-books are made just for teachers. The Association for Supervision and Curriculum Development (ASCD) hosts a teacher library with six books on classroom management and instruction that can be read online. The Center for Applied Special Technology (CAST) has an excellent online book, *Teaching Every Student in the Digital Age* (Figure 9.6), with resource hyperlinks, extra activities, background research, and more. The National Academies Press has more than 2,000 texts available for online reading in a variety of areas, including more than 200 books in education— one is the educational bestseller *How People Learn*. It's even possible to find educational classics such as John Dewy's *Democracy and Education*, which can be downloaded in multiple formats from the Blackmask Online library.

Figure 9.6. CAST's *Teaching Every Student in the Digital Age* online e-book has resource hyperlinks, extra activities, and background research.

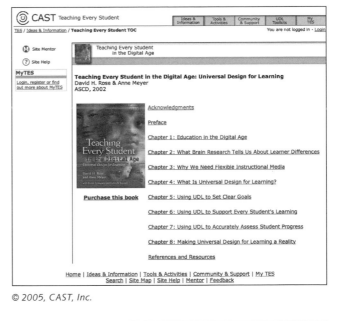

© 2005, CAST, Inc.

ASCD Full-Text Books:
www.ascd.org/cms/index.cfm?TheViewID=652
Six complete books on education and educational issues.

Blackmask Online:
www.blackmask.com
A user-supported library of texts in categories ranging from biography to poetry to nonfiction.

CAST: www.cast.org/products/
Two universal access/technology education books with only the text of the book online, but also enriched with multimedia examples of UDL as well a number of interactive tutorials, tools, and templates. The books are *Learning to Read in the Computer Age* and *Teaching Every Student in the Digital Age.*

National Academies Press: www.nap.edu/browse.html
More than 2,000 professional books (including an education section) that can be read online, including *How People Learn.*

National Institute for Literacy: www.nifl.gov/nifl/publications.html
Online books about reading, including *Put Reading First: The Research Building Blocks for Teaching Children to Read.*

Figure 9.7. eBookLocator is a specialized e-book search engine.

© 2005 OverDrive, Inc.

Search Tools

If the previous lists of electronic libraries don't have what you want, you can also look for e-books using specialized e-book search engines, such as the eBook-Locator (Figure 9.7) and the Online Books Page, as well as general search engines, such as MSN and Yahoo. Search engines can find e-books on Web sites that have only one or two e-books for distribution and may not be associated with an online library. The Google search engine has started scanning millions of books and periodicals from libraries, such as the New York Public Library and the Harvard, University of Michigan, and Oxford libraries, into an e-book collection called Google Print. During any search, the Google search engine may identify a book that fits within the given search parameter. The book will be identified by a book icon in the search results. By clicking on the link, a searcher will have access to the book. In the case of copyrighted works, access will be limited to an abstract or a single page. If the work is in the public domain, the entire work will be accessible.

Specialized E-book Search Engines

Digital Book Index: www.digitalbookindex.com/search001a.htm
This indexes most major e-book sites, along with thousands of smaller specialized sites.

eBookLocator: www.ebooklocator.com
Search database of thousands of books.

Google Books: http://print.goggle.com
This is a Google digitized book service.

Google Scholar: http://scholar.google.com/
Google provides this tool to search scholarly papers.

The Online Books Page: http://onlinebooks.library.upenn.edu/
Search from more than 20,000 listings.

SearcheBooks: www.searchebooks.com
Searche-books searches multiple full textbook sites.

General Search Engines

Google: www.google.com

MSN Search: http://search.msn.com

Yahoo: www.yahoo.com

Conducting a Readability Analysis

Once a teacher has found e-books to use in class, he or she may wish to determine the reading level of the material to assess its appropriateness for the students. Readability is especially important for struggling readers, according to Allington (2001). There should be a correlation between the student's reading level and the book's readability level. Eighty percent of a student's books should be at a level that the student can read independently, meaning one or two grades below the student's tested level, and 20% should be at instructional level, the student's current tested reading level.

Figure 9.8. Textalyser is a readability analysis tool.

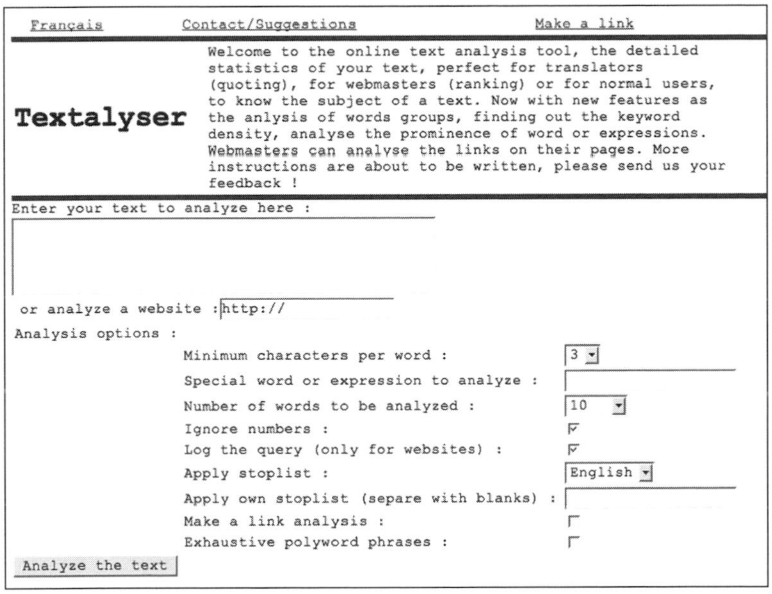

Readability can be assessed with a readily available computer analysis. Electronic text and e-books are easily analyzed for readability because the text can be dragged and dropped into a readability program. Educators can analyze a portion of an e-book or even an entire e-book. Some great tools are Using English.com, OKAPI!, and Textalyser (Figure 9.8).

Educators can use readability statistics to track student growth in reading. Some readability tools will determine a grade level for the material. Using these methods educators can collect banks of e-books and articles appropriate for student use.

Microsoft Word's Readability Statistics Analyzer

Many are unaware that Microsoft Word has a readability statistics analyzer built into the word processor. Word will analyze written material using the Flesch-Kincaid model, which provides a grade level between 0 and 12 and reading ease between 0% and 100% (Figure 9.9). The Flesch Reading Ease calculation rates the document's text on a 100-point scale; the higher the score, the easier it is to understand the document. For most standard documents, people aim for a score of approximately 60% to 70%.

To complete a readability analysis on an e-book using Word, select an online e-book in HTML or text format and open it in Word. Or, highlight portions of an e-book or article, copy it, and paste it into a blank Word document. Now that the text is in Word, make sure the readability function is turned on. To do this, follow these steps:

1. On the **Tools** menu, select the **Spelling and Grammar** tab.

2. Make sure that the **Check grammar** box is checked.

3. Select Options, then select the **Show readability statistics** check box. Click **OK**.

4. Now run a spelling and grammar check on the document.

5. From this point on, every time spelling and grammar are checked, Word will also display the readability statistics of the document.

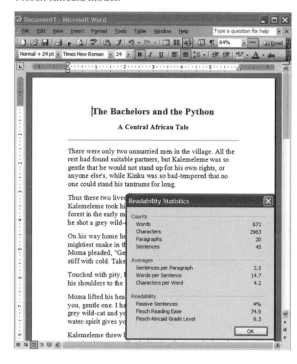

Figure 9.9. MS Word analyzes the readability of the Central Afrian folktale *The Bachelors and the Python*, using the Flesch-Kincaid model.

Following is a real-life example of how useful readability statistics can be.

In the Classroom

Mr. Deneb's middle school team has decided that all teachers will include narrative story reading in their classes. Mr. Deneb is currently teaching about world biomes, so he wants to include high-interest stories about animals to supplement the current course work. He decides to use the Tales of Wonder site (www.darsie.net/talesofwonder/index.html), which has folk tales from 14 regions around the world. The tales include a number of animal stories.

The site has a section of stories from central Africa, which feature the tropical savanna biome. Mr. Deneb reads through a few of the stories and selects an interesting story that mentions climate elements. Since the stories are short, he highlights the entire story, copies it, and pastes it into a blank Word document. Then he runs a spelling and grammar check on the document. When it is complete, he gets a pop-up window with the story's readability statistics (Figure 9.9).

Mr. Deneb finds that the reading level of the story *The Bachelors and the Python* is relatively close to his students' grade level, with a Flesch-Kincaid score of 6.3 (meaning three months into the sixth grade) and a Flesch Reading Ease of 74.9 (meaning a relatively easy read). Mr. Deneb also works with the team's social studies teacher, sharing the site with her and planning when the stories will be read, so that the social studies teacher can teach about the culture of the region from which the story comes.

Text Analysis Tools

OKAPI!: www.interventioncentral.org/
htmdocs/tools/okapi/okapi.shtml
OKAPI! performs Dale-Chall or Spache
readability analyses or creates
curriculum-based assessment probes.

Readability Test: www.juicystudio.com/fog/
This site calculates the Gunning Fog Index,
Flesch Reading Ease, and Flesch-Kincaid
for HTML files.

Textalyser: http://textalyser.net/
Textalyser calculates the Gunning Fog
Index and lexical density.

Text Content Analysis Tool:
www.usingenglish.com/resources/
text-statistics.php
This site calculates the Gunning Fog Index
and lexical density.

Using English.com: www.usingenglish.com/
resources/text-statistics.php
Statistics provided include word count, unique words, number of sentences,
average words per sentence, lexical density, and the Gunning Fog Index.

[**Lesson**Idea]

Reading Assessment

From an e-book, select reading passages to use as a reading assessment (up to 170 words). Copy the passage and go to the OPAKI! site (www.interventioncentral.org/htmdocs/tools/okapi/okapi.shtml) to create a curriculum-based reading probe. Have the student read the analyzed pages aloud for one minute to find the number of words read correct. This is a highly reliable measure of general reading achievement.

Conclusion

With thousands of e-books available in so many formats on so many subjects, the odds are good that educators will find e-books for their students. Make sure to browse the various stores and libraries to find something for your students to read or use as a reference.

Reference

Allington, R. (2001). *What really matters for struggling readers: Designing research-based programs.*
New York: Longman.

Chapter 10

Creating Your Own E-books

You don't have to rely on bookstores and libraries for useful e-books—you can easily create your own. Teachers can create e-books as research or reading material for the home or classroom. More and more teachers are exchanging traditional print materials for e-book files because of their distribution ease, interactions, and reading supports. Others are creating e-books for use by students with special needs (chapter 8).

This chapter focuses on creating text e-books in the big five formats (chapter 3), as well as in presentation software and iPod notes formats. The big five formats are plain text, HTML, Adobe Reader, Microsoft Reader, and eReader (formerly Palm Reader).

Creating E-books for School Projects

E-book creation can be associated with many school projects. Students can create e-books as part of a writing activity, for themselves or others. Older students can create reading material for younger students as part of a class project or for volunteer credit.

Students can also create e-books as class assignments when they are learning about the writing process, such as in Writer's Workshop. Writer's Workshop is an interdisciplinary writing technique that builds students' abilities in the writing process. Using Writer's Workshop, an educator makes the writing process a meaningful part of the classroom curriculum. In this process, students choose their topic, develop a story or other material on the topic, and then share their creations. Planning, editing, revising, and using correct grammar are all components of Writer's Workshop (Teachersfirst, 2003).

There are several advantages to having students create their own e-books. One is that students are already interested in using technology, and this process can get students excited about writing. Another advantage is that once the e-book is created, the digital form adds an additional dimension of wider distribution. Educators can use student-created e-books to create digital libraries of student work. The student e-books can be shared with the class or with the world if the student's work is published through a class or school Web site. E-books can also be used to supplement a student's portfolio.

Figure 10.1. The Stories for the Heart site presents e-books written by middle school students as part of a project on the writing process.

© 2003–04. St. Elizabeth School, Grades 5 and 6 students, Ottawa, Canada.

In the Classroom

An example of one class creating and sharing their e-books can be found at the Web site Stories for the Heart (www.occdsb.on.ca/~sel/literacy/heart/heart_index.htm; see Figure 10.1). Students in this sixth-grade class created e-books for themselves and younger students as a way to learn about the writing process. The students worked in cooperative groups to create stories about values for first-graders. After choosing a specific topic, the students brainstormed and used graphic organizers to develop their ideas into a rough story concept. Then they worked out drafts of their stories on paper, revising and editing as they developed their ideas. They also created hand-drawn illustrations relating to their stories.

Next, each group used a word processor to create a typed version of their story. They also scanned the drawn images and inserted them into the document. Paper copies of the books were created and taken to the lower grades for a cooperative reading activity between the classes. Using MS Word, the students converted the word processing files into MS Reader e-book files, which were then posted on the school's Web site to expand the audience beyond the school.

Sample quotes published on the Stories for the Heart site include:

"This project really made us learn about the writing process."

"I really liked the scanning and trying to fit the pictures into the stories."

"I thought it was cool to see my pictures and words on the site."

Meeting the Standards

Creating their own e-books also allows students to address a number of technology and language arts standards, such as the following.

ISTE National Educational Technology Standards for Students (NETS•S)

1. Basic operations and concepts

    ■   Students are proficient in the use of technology.

3. Technology productivity tools

    ■   Students use technology tools to enhance learning, increase productivity, and promote creativity.

    ■   Students use productivity tools to collaborate in constructing technology-enhanced models, preparing publications, and producing other creative works.

4. Technology communications tools

    ■   Students use telecommunications to collaborate, publish, and interact with peers, experts, and other audiences.

    ■   Students use a variety of media and formats to communicate information and ideas effectively to multiple audiences. (ISTE, 1998)

Standards for the English Language Arts

4. Students adjust their use of spoken, written, and visual language (e.g., conventions, style, vocabulary) to communicate effectively with a variety of audiences and for different purposes.

5. Students employ a wide range of strategies as they write and use different writing process elements appropriately to communicate with different audiences for a variety of purposes.

8. Students use a variety of technological and information resources (e.g., libraries, databases, computer networks, video) to gather and synthesize information and to create and communicate knowledge.

12. Students use spoken, written, and visual language to accomplish their own purposes (e.g., for learning, enjoyment, persuasion, and the exchange of information). (NCTE & IRA, 1996)

Reprinted with permission from Standards for the English Language Arts, p. 24. Copyright © 1996 by the International Reading Association and the National Council of Teachers of English. All rights reserved.

First Steps to E-book Creation

Many tools are available for creating text-format e-books, including common application software and free programs dedicated to creating or converting existing electronic text material into e-books. Standard application software, such as word processing or presentation software, can be used to create e-books from scratch. Plug-ins for word processors are available that convert documents into e-books, and specialized software can convert documents, text, or Web pages into e-books. Educators can add notes, organizers, comments, and questions to text before converting it to an e-book format for student use.

The following sections describe how to make e-books in the big five formats of text, HTML, Adobe Reader, MS Reader, and eReader, and how to create talking e-books using PowerPoint. iPod Notes are also discussed.

The first step in e-books creation is usually importing or typing text into a text editor, such as a word processor, or using a scanner running optical character recognition (OCR) software. When scanning a book, the OCR software may produce errors that aren't detected by a spelling checker. For example, the word "clear" could be identified by the scanning software as "dear," so it's important to proofread all scanned material. If the author hand wrote the book's text, it might be easier and faster to type the text rather than scan it.

When creating your own e-book, you will determine the length: it can be a few pages or span several chapters. If you're converting one of the many epublic domain text files on the Internet, be aware that while the work itself is public domain, the format in which the text is presented on the Web page is not. This means that the words on the site are public domain but the coding, such as HTML, is copyrighted.

[Lesson**Idea**]

Upper/Lower Grades Stories Sharing

Have upper grade students write stories based on a theme. Transfer the stories to a word processor, then use an e-books creation program to convert the word processing documents into e-books. Have the students take their e-books to classes in lower grades and read them their stories.

Creating Plain Text E-books

Perhaps the simplest form of e-book is the plain text e-book. Text e-books are usually either in text (TXT) or rich text format (RTF), but they can be in other document formats as well. The tool for creating text e-books is any word processor. Here's the procedure: Open the book text in the word processor window. Save the file in either text or rich text format. Saving the e-book as a plain text file means that the e-book will contain only unformatted text, not pictures or special font formatting. To include images and other features in the e-book, save the file in rich text format.

Text e-books can be read with word processors, Web browsers, and special e-book readers, such as Tom's eTextReader for the PC, which can also perform as a pure text e-book editor (Figure 10.2).

Figure 10.2. Tom's eTextReader displays and edits plain text e-books on a PC.

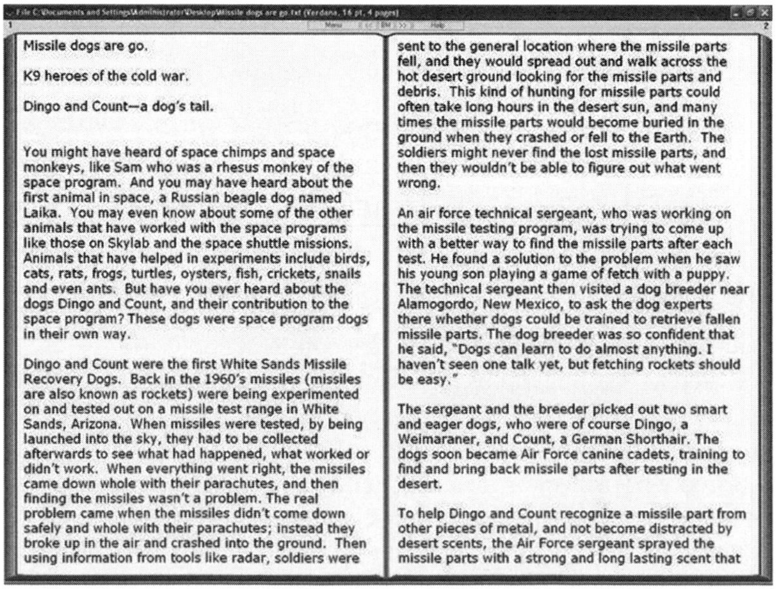

Figure 10.3. HTML e-books can be created with a Web editor such as FrontPage.

Creating HTML E-books

E-books can also easily be created using a Web editor, such as Microsoft FrontPage, Dreamweaver, Netscape Communicator, or any number of other Web editor programs, many of which are available online for free. HTML e-books can also be created using a word processor program by using the **Save as HTML...** or **Save as Web page...** option. Most current word processors offer this option.

Using a Web editor is usually easy and doesn't require learning HTML code, although it could be helpful. To use the Web editor, write text and insert pictures as with a word processor (Figure 10.3). With a Web editor, you can format the placement of images, the size and structure of text, and even the background color.

Creating Adobe Reader E-books

Unless you have a program such as Adobe Acrobat, you will be creating the e-book material in one format and converting it to PDF. If you have the full Adobe Acrobat program (not Acrobat Reader or Adobe Reader) you can get details on e-book creation by downloading the e-book *How to Create Adobe PDF E-books* from Adobe at www.adobe.com/epaper/tips/acr5e-book/pdfs/e-book.pdf. With Macintosh computers running OS X and some word processors, such as OpenOffice, you can export or save documents as PDF files (Figure 10.4). In this case, using the word processor, the e-book is written and saved in a document format and then exported. The program creates another version of the document in PDF format.

If your word processor can't create PDF files directly, an online converter can be used. Online conversion programs convert text files and word-processed documents into PDF files. BCL Technologies (goBCL.com) hosts a free document conversion service

Figure 10.4. OpenOffice's Export to PDF option will save your file as a PDF e-book.

Figure 10.5. BCL Technologies offers an online document converter for PDFs.

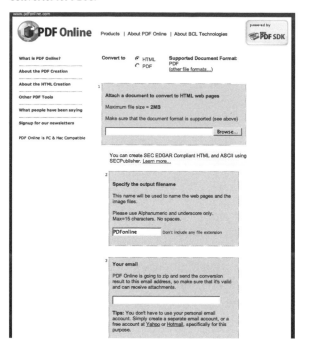

at www.gobcl.com/convert_pdf.asp and offers a variety of document formats (Figure 10.5). The Web site runs a program, converts the files, zip compresses the created files, and e-mails them to the given address.

Creating MS Reader E-books

MS Reader e-books can be created in two relatively simple ways: by using Microsoft's Word with a special plug-in, or by using a ReaderWorks program. In both cases the documents are converted to Web pages and then to MS Reader e-book files (LIT). Both techniques allow you to integrate images (JPEG, GIF, and PNG) into the e-book and generate a table of contents.

Creating e-books for MS Reader using Word 2000 or above is a straightforward process. First, download and run the Read in Microsoft Reader (RMR) plug-in, available from the Microsoft Reader site at www.microsoft.com/reader/developers/downloads/rmr.asp (Figure 10.6). After the plug-in is downloaded and installed, a new feature is added to Word's **File** menu, **Read...**, which will convert the Word document temporarily into a Web page and then finally into an MS Reader e-book. To create an e-book with the RMR plug-in:

1. Create the text.

2. Edit the text using Word.

3. Save the e-book as a Word document.

4. Go to the **File** menu and select the **Read...** option.

5. Fill in the information in the Read in Microsoft Reader pop-up window. Identify the title, author, filename, location, and then decide whether a table of contents is needed and whether cover art is desired.

6. Click the **OK** button to create the e-book file.

Figure 10.6. The Read in Microsoft Reader plug-in can be downloaded to create e-books.

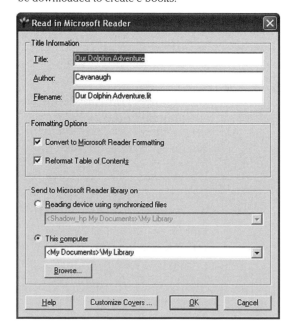

Figure 10.7. ReaderWorks Standard is a free program to create e-books in LIT format.

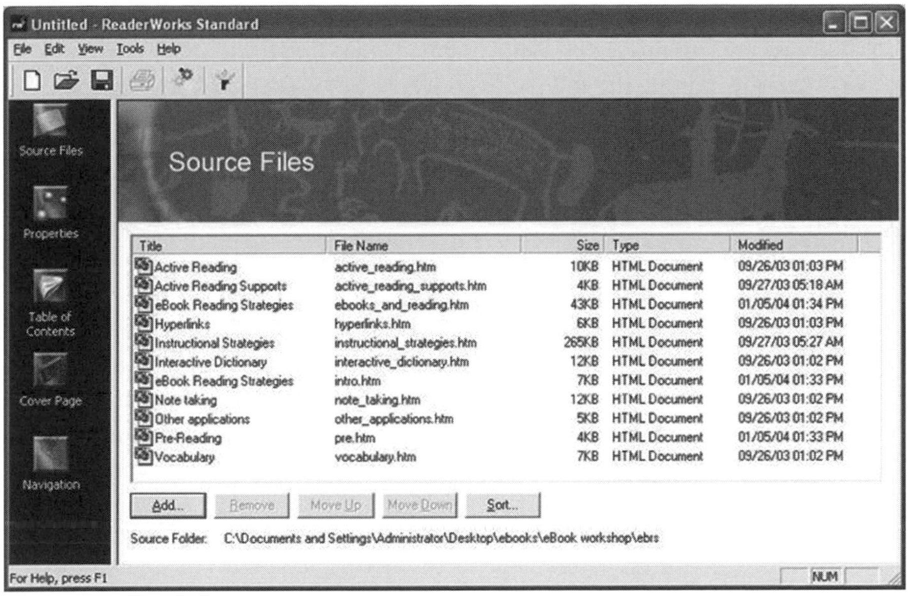

© 2005 OverDrive, Inc.

Another program, ReaderWorks (www.overdrive.com), also creates e-books in the MS Reader (LIT) format. ReaderWorks is available in a Standard (free) version and a Professional (not free) version. It allows users to convert documents saved as Web pages into the MS Reader format (Figure 10.7). To create an e-book with ReaderWorks:

1. Create the text.

2. Edit the text using a word processor or an HTML editor.

3. Save the soon-to-be e-book in its own folder. The ReaderWorks program will create a number of files when it's making the e-book, so saving all the material in a single folder simplifies the process.

4. Start the ReaderWorks program.

5. Add the HTML files to the Source files section either through the **Add** button or using drag and drop.

6. Set the properties, identifying the text, author, date, and so on.

7. Make a table of contents.

8. Save your project using **Save As** and the RWP extension. This will save the e-book project, not the e-book itself. This way if the e-book isn't right, you can open the project and make changes and then create the e-book again.

9. Go to the **File** menu and choose **Build e-book**. Watch as ReaderWorks creates the e-book.

If you are creating a chapter book or longer document, you may wish to have each chapter start on a new page. To do this you must add HTML code to the header of the Web document. First, go though the text and set the chapter title to have a heading level of 2. Next, open the Web page's HTML code, adding the following code just before the </head> tag to cause all headings at level 2 to begin on a new page. Then use ReaderWorks as described.

```
<style>
<!--
H1, H2, H3, H4, H5, H6 {
page-break-before: auto; /* the default */
page-break-inside: avoid; /* no page breaks inside... */
page-break-after: avoid; /* ... or after */
}
H2 {
page-break-before: always; /* begin new chapters; overrides previous rule */
}
P {
orphans: 3; /* default is 2 */
widows: 3; /* default is 2 */
-->
</style>
```

Creating eReader E-books

The Web site eReader.com offers a free program titled DropBook that converts a text file coded with Palm Markup Language (PML) tags into an eReader e-book for use on Palm and Pocket PC handheld devices as well as Macintosh and Windows desktops. To learn about the Palm Markup Language, visit eReader.com at www.ereader.com/dropbook.

Coding Word Documents with Palm Markup Language

It's possible to code a Microsoft Word document with the Palm Markup format, without learning PML, by using a downloadable Word template that has a special macro. Download the zip compressed Word template document, word2pml.zip, from www.drscavanaugh. org/ebooks/word2pml.zip and unzip the file. Then place the word2pml.dot file into the computer's Word template folder. To mark up the document with the PML code, follow these steps for a PC (where Mac instructions vary, they appear in parentheses):

1. Run Word. From the **File** menu, choose **New...** .

2. From the list of available templates, choose **word2PML** and click **OK**. (On a Mac, choose **Open...** , find the template file, and open it.)

Figure 10.8. This Word document is coded with PML after running the Word2PML macro.

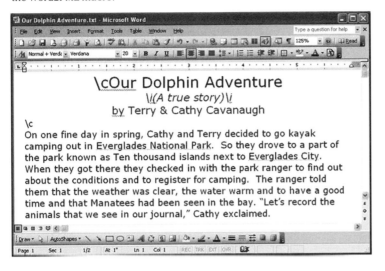

3. The screen should now display a blank document. Copy and paste in the text that you wish to code to the PML format.

4. From the **Tools** menu, choose **Macro**. (On a Mac, from the **Tools** menu, choose **Macro**, then **Macros…**) The macros pop-up should now display.

5. Scroll down the macros list and select the word2PML macro, then click **Run**. Running the macro places the PML code into the document (Figure 10.8).

6. Create a subfolder for the images within the folder containing the text document. This subfolder needs to have the same name as the text document but with "_img" added to the name (example tarzan_img as the subfolder name).

7. Add the book images to the subfolder. Images must be in ping (PNG) format and need to be either black and white or 8-bit color (256 color). In the coded document, add the code statement **/m="name.png"** (include the quote marks) for each image you want to have included in the book.

8. Save the file as a plain text (TXT) document.

Running DropBook

Creating an eReader (PDB) e-book file is a matter of dragging and dropping a text file that has been coded with the Palm Markup Language. Start the DropBook program, then drag the file's icon and drop it onto the DropBook window (Figure 10.9). A pop-up window will then ask for the title, author, publisher, copyright, and ISBN number. At a minimum the title must be entered, and then the program will convert the text into the e-book file (Figure 10.10).

Creating E-books with Presentation Software

Using a common presentation tool, such as Microsoft PowerPoint, teachers and students can create their own talking electronic books. E-books in a presentation program such as

Figure 10.9. Use the DropBook program to build the book by dragging and dropping the TXT file onto the DropBook icon or window.

Figure 10.10. This eReader e-book was created with DropBook.

PowerPoint don't have to be converted to an e-book format—the presentation file itself is the e-book.

Presentation e-books can be "played" on a computer or printed and bound. Another classroom application is to create digital "big books" for class reading and other activities. By using a video projector or large-screen television connected to an online computer, a teacher can display the book to the whole class to use as an instructional reading activity, or to exhibit examples of writing, culture, or art. These digital big books would not by themselves cost anything extra, and they have the added advantage of being able to be placed onto a disc and made available outside class, including at a student's home.

The easiest way to start creating your presentation e-book is to create a folder in which to store all your files and then create a template to use for your e-book. A PowerPoint e-book template is available from the Drs. Cavanaugh e-book Web site (www.drscavanaugh.org/ebooks/) that can be used to get started on a PowerPoint e-book.

The reason to use a template (whether you download it or create your own), is to save time later. With a template you won't have to repeatedly add items such as page turners to the book pages.

If PowerPoint isn't available, try downloading and using OpenOffice's presentation tool. OpenOffice is a free productivity suite of tools, available from www.openoffice.org.

Creating E-books for the iPod

It's even possible to create an e-book for the iPod, not as audio but as text. Using an online program at the iPod e-book Creator site (www.ambience.sk/ipod-e-book-creator/ipod-book-notes-text-conversion.php) upload a plain text e-book file, such as those created with a word processor or from Project Gutenberg. The online program will then convert the text file into a notes file for download to a local computer. The program creates notes for use with an iPod's Notes function. Unzip the downloaded file and then transfer it to the iPod. The e-book is now ready for viewing.

Other software programs for both Windows and Macintosh platforms can convert e-books to iPod notes. The iStory Creator can be used to build "choose your own ending" text game stories; iPodLibrary for the PC will convert major e-book formats for the iPod; and Book2Pod for the Mac will convert text files to iPod e-books. The manybooks.net (www.manybooks.net) online library provides more than 600 e-book titles for free download in the iPod Notes format.

Conclusion

Choose a format or two and try creating some e-books. After you've made a few, you'll be surprised at how easy it is. Allowing students to create e-books can be a practical and insightful technology learning activity and provide valuable material for your classroom. Creating more high-interest reading material for your students can expand your classroom resources for years to come.

Online Resources

Adobe Reader Books

How to Create Adobe PDF E-books: www.adobe.com/epaper/tips/acr5ebook/pdfs/eBook.pdf
Adobe has written this e-book to explain how to create Adobe PDF e-books.

eReader Books

MS Word Plug-in for Palm Markup: www.drscavanaugh.org/ebooks/word2pml.zip
This plug-in converts documents in Word by adding Palm Markup Language [PML] code.

Palm DropBook: www.ereader.com/dropbook/download
This onverter creates eReader e-books.

Palm Markup Language: www.palmdigitalmedia.com/dropbook/pml
PML is a coding system for creating eReader e-books.

iPod Books

Book2Pod: www.tomsci.com/book2pod/
Book2Pod converts text files into iPod notes for the Mac.

manybooks.net: www.manybooks.net
Mmore than 600 books in a variety of formats, including iPod notes, are offered.

iPod e-book Creator: www.ambience.sk/ipod-e-book-creator/ipod-book-notes-text-conversion.php
The Creator converts text files into iPod notes.

iPodLibrary: http://sturm.t35.com/ipodlibrary/
iPodLibrary imports major e-book formats [LIT, PDF, HTML, TXT] into the iPod for Windows.

iStory Creator: www.ipodsoft.com/index.php?/software/istory
This tool creates linked file stories, such as "choose your own ending stories," for the iPod for Mac and Windows.

MS Reader Books

MS Word RMR Plug-in: www.microsoft.com/reader/developers/downloads/rmr.asp
This plug-in converts Word documents into MS Reader e-books.

ReaderWorks: www.overdrive.com
Standard (free) and professional (not free) versions are available to create MS Reader e-books.

Additional Software

goBCL.com: www.gobcl.com/convert_pdf.asp
   This provides document conversion to HTML and Adobe PDF format.

Netscape Communicator (Web page editor that creates HTML documents):
   www.netscape.com

OpenOffice: www.openoffice.org
   This word processor creates PDF, TXT, and HTML documents.

Tom's eTextReader: http://pws.prserv.net/Fellner/Software/eTR.htm
   This e-book reader program displays plain text files in a book-like manner.

Student-Created E-books

Stories for the Heart: www.occdsb.on.ca/~sel/literacy/heart/heart_index.htm

References

Teachersfirst.com. (2003). *Writer's workshop: Making writing a lifelong habit for elementary students.* Retrieved November 2004 from www.teachersfirst.com/lessons/writers/index.html

International Society for Technology in Education (ISTE). (1998). *National educational technology standards for students.* Eugene, OR: Author. Also available online at http://cnets.iste.org/students/s-_stands.html

The National Council of Teachers of English & the International Reading Association (NCTE & IRA). (1996). *Standards for the English language arts.* Urbana, IL: Author. Retrieved May 2005 from www.ncte.org/about/over/standards/110846.htm

Chapter  Building a Digital Library

The International Reading Association has called for increased funding for books for classroom, school, and community libraries. "Libraries should include storybooks, novels, biography, fiction and nonfiction material, magazines, poetry, and a multitude of other types of print materials to suit the interests and range of reading abilities of all children" (IRA, 2000, p. 1). Unfortunately for most classrooms and schools, the funding isn't there.

The IRA (1999) also recommends at least seven books per student in a classroom library, and the selection of books needs to change periodically.

E-books can help meet both needs. For little to no cost, using technologies already available at most schools, it's possible to expand the school library or media center's collection of books and at the same time make many of these new books more accessible for students. Using Internet libraries gives teachers and students greater access to books, without adding to the teacher's or library's book budget, or taking up additional shelf space.

Some reasons to have e-books available in the library or media center include:

- E-books don't take up shelf space.

- E-books don't need to be reshelved.

- The book budget isn't affected (when using free resources).

- Public domain e-books are free and don't have to be returned.

- E-books can more easily be accessed by students at home.

The addition of e-books to school libraries, especially at the upper levels (Grades 6–12), allows libraries to provide support for teachers and students by housing and distributing books that are used in classes. Most of what is considered classic literature, such as the works of Shakespeare, has passed into the public domain, and school libraries can freely give digital copies to students, to have and to keep.

Integrating e-books into a school media center or library is usually done either by signing up for a subscription service or by creating the school's own digital e-book collection. This new library, an "e-library," is used differently by patrons. Instead of taking the hardcopy book out of the library, readers check out the e-book either by accessing it for online reading or by downloading it for offline reading. This digital library can be open to students and families at all hours through the Internet or from every classroom through the school's intranet.

Subscription Library Services

By subscribing to an e-book library service, users have access to the collection 24 hours a day, seven days a week, through the Internet. Subscribers purchase a collection of e-book titles just as they would purchase print titles, but usually also pay a service fee.

Two services that provide collections of pre-leveled books include Reading A–Z (www. readinga-z.com) and childrenselibrary.com (Figure 11.1). The multimedia e-books from childrenselibrary are designed to be read online, while the Reading A–Z books are designed to be downloaded and printed.

Figure 11.1. The childrenselibrary.com Web site offers multimedia e-books designed to be read online.

Printed with permission of childrenselibrary (chidlrenselibrary.com).

As with print books, only one student at a time may access each purchased copy of an e-book. The library or media center sets the checkout time for each e-book, typically a few hours. Timed checkout of e-book files can be managed with Adobe's Content Server, among other programs. Depending on the system and e-book files, readers will use either a browser or platform-specific e-book program to read the e-books. E-books on a timed checkout will no longer be displayed until checked out again.

Subscription library fees are usually based on the volume of books requested, with additional service fees. Subscription services provide reporting tools and usage statistics. The e-books are usually provided with full MARC records and can be incorporated into a library's existing Integrated Library System (ILS). (See box on next page for descriptions of these terms.)

By using an online subscription service, a library or media center can quickly add thousands of titles to its collection, without having to add any shelves for the new books. Other benefits of using a subscription e-book service include no lost, stolen, or overdue books. The e-library subscription vendors currently available include:

childrenselibrary: childrenselibrary.com

netLibrary: www.netlibrary.com/Gateway.aspx

ebrary: www.ebrary.com/index.jsp
(Figure 11.2)

Questia: www.questia.com/Index.jsp

OverDrive—Digital Library Reserve:
www.overdrive.com

Reading A–Z: www.readinga-z.com

Special Needs Subscriptions

Another form of subscription service is available for students with special needs. Companies such as Bookshare.org (www.bookshare.org) and the Accessible Book Collection (www.accessiblebook collection.org) provide an important service to schools and students by offering digital text to qualified persons with special needs, such as low vision, blindness, reading disabilities, dyslexia, and mobility impairments. For more information, see chapter 8.

MARC
(**MA**chine-**R**eadable **C**ataloging)

MARC is a communications standard for library holdings and other data. The data found in the MARC records make up the base elements found in most library catalogs.

ILS
(**I**ntegrated **L**ibrary **S**ystem)

An ILS is a technology system used to automate the primary functions of a library, such as ordering, cataloging, and circulation. The ILS goes beyond a card catalog, keeping track of all library items, including which person has which book checked out and when it should be returned.

Figure 11.2. ebrary is one of several useful subscription sites for digital books.

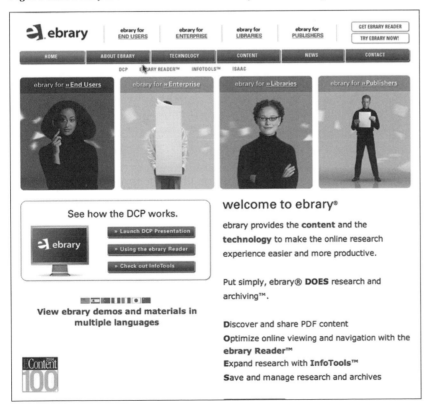

Creating Your Own E-library

You can create your own e-library, instead of or in addition to subscribing to a service. To construct an e-library, simply collect the e-books, store them on a computer or server, catalogue them, and then make them available to the students. Books with copyrights from before the 1920s are classified as public domain books and can be downloaded, converted, and distributed openly.

Here are some questions to consider when constructing your e-library.

Where will the e-library be housed? Digital libraries can be housed on a stand-alone computer, on a CD, added to the school network, or placed on the Internet.

Does my school have Internet Web space? If yes, you can make your e-library available to students, their families, and the world for download and reading. If not, students will only have access to the books you place on your school network, a stand-alone computer, or a CD.

Can students access the school network or Internet from computers in the classroom? If not, students who need to download books will have to go to a stand-alone location such as the school library or access an e-library on CD.

How can I make access easy for students? If students will be accessing the e-library through the school's intranet or the Internet, create a page of links on the library's Web site. These links should connect to the e-book files either on your library's server or on another library's server. If you are constructing a stand-alone or CD e-library, download all the books into a folder or series of folders. Then, create an interface, such as an HTML page with hyperlinks, for easy access to the e-book files from the computer or disc. Both options allow students to download the files onto portable media, such as flash cards or jump drives.

Steps to Constructing an E-library

Use the following steps as guidelines when constructing your own e-library.

1. Decide whether you want to have links to e-books in other libraries or would prefer to have the e-books files located locally. If you are connecting to other libraries, there is a chance that the library link will change. Also, the book files might not be compatible with your users' devices or software. Consider that your school system's access to the Internet may not always be available. If you decide to publish the books on the Internet, they will be accessible to users to either read online or download 24 hours a day. Libraries without Internet access can make e-book files available on an intranet, school network, CD, or stand-alone computer e-library station.

2. Evaluate and select books that match or support the school reading lists and curricula. To do this you will need a compiled reading list and a catalog of common curriculum topics. Then you will need to peruse the existing public domain libraries for books you can use. Even if you have print copies of a particular book in your collection, you may want to obtain e-book copies, especially as public domain e-books are ones you can give away without worrying about their return. Consider going beyond the required reading list to include other books by required authors.

3. Convert your books to the needed formats (see the following section and chapter 10 for more information). Start by downloading the sharable e-books in as many formats as possible, and then convert them to other desired formats. It's good to provide e-books in

multiple formats to ensure that they are readable with familiar or available tools, especially for home use. Try for all of the big five e-book formats (plain text, HTML, Adobe Reader, MS Reader, and eReader) and any other that you might want.

4. Create a Web site with links to each of your collection's e-book files. This Web site method will work even for offline book browsing. Any computer browser will display a Web page, even if it's not connected to the Internet. A more advanced option is to create a database of the e-book files, and then link it with a Web authoring system (ASP or PHP). E-book databases can be stored in several places, such as on the school's Web server, on a file server, or on a database server such as SQL or Oracle.

5. Don't forget to include links to reader software on the library site. If you are creating a stand-alone computer station, install software for all the formats on that computer. If you are creating an e-book library CD, make sure to download the reader installation files onto the CD.

6. Publish your collection: Place your e-book e-library on your computer system or on CDs so that everyone has access.

It's possible to buy a complete e-book library and then use it as the base on which to build your own. For example, Blackmask Online (www.blackmask.com/catalo/default.php) sells DVD copies of its 12,000 copyright-free books for about $30 per e-book format. You can use the book files from that DVD to start your library's e-book collection. A benefit of using books that have passed into the public domain is that they can be given to students at no cost without worry of return. Baen Science Fiction (www.baen.com) includes a large number of its current titles on CD for free sharing if you buy their hardbacks with the CD inside. Remember not to share files unless you have permission or they are in the public domain.

Making E-books for Your Collection

No costly tools are needed to convert existing electronic text into e-book formats. Microsoft, for instance, provides a free plug-in for Word that allows users to change any Word document into an e-book file formatted for the Microsoft Reader. eReader.com (formerly Palm) has a similar system with DropBook, which is a program for Windows and Macintosh that allows conversion of a text file to the Palm Markup Language for reading with the eReader. In addition to using the converters to make your book available in different formats, you can use them to add original student writing to your e-book library. See chapter 10 for more information.

Accreditation and Standards

While current school accreditation requirements don't specifically mention e-books, the books could be considered part of the media center resources category. According to the school accreditation agencies recognized by the U.S. Department of Education, school

---

[**Lesson**Idea]

MP3 Library

Place student-created audio books as MP3 files onto the school or class Web site for download. Students can then download the books to listen to using their MP3 players.

library or media collections should consist of a balance of print, nonprint, and electronic media adequate and appropriate in quality and quantity to support the school's curriculum. Contact the regional accrediting organizations for more information; their contact information is listed in the next section.

The International Reading Association has issued a policy statement concerning library and media centers stating that there should be a "minimum of two books per child purchased each year for school libraries and a minimum of one new book per year for classrooms" (IRA, 1999). E-books provide to schools alternatives to print material, and also allow libraries to expand their collections without taking up additional space.

While some of the school accreditation agencies do not yet consider e-books as books, all the agencies contacted by the author have indicated that they plan to revisit such technology advancements in their standards.

The use of e-books as tools for students in the classroom assists students in achieving technology standards developed by ISTE (1998). For students, e-books address a number of the NETS·S areas including:

2. **Social, ethical, and human issues:** Students develop positive attitudes toward technology uses that support lifelong learning, collaboration, personal pursuits, and productivity.

3. **Technology productivity tools:** Students use productivity tools to collaborate in constructing technology-enhanced models, preparing publications, and producing other creative works.

4. **Technology communications tools:** Students use telecommunications to collaborate, publish, and interact with peers, experts, and other audiences.

5. **Technology research tools:** Students use technology to locate, evaluate, and collect information from a variety of sources.

Students using e-books develop their understanding of electronic text technology and its applications, and they can apply these abilities to improving their learning, communication, and research abilities. As new e-book features continue to be developed, such as the annotation function, students will be able to more effectively interact with the technology for research.

The application of e-books in the school setting also addresses ISTE's NETS for Teachers, or NETS·T (2000). The following standards apply:

II. **Planning and Designing Learning Environments and Experiences**

C. Teachers identify and locate technology resources and evaluate them for accuracy and suitability.

V. **Productivity and Professional Practice**

A. Teachers use technology resources to engage in ongoing professional development and lifelong learning.

    D.   Teachers use technology to communicate and collaborate with peers, parents, and the larger community in order to nurture student learning.

VI. Social, Ethical, Legal, and Human Issues

    B.   Teachers apply technology resources to enable and empower learners with diverse backgrounds, characteristics, and abilities.

Teachers using electronic text applications develop their abilities by applying such technologies to create more effective learning opportunities. They can implement technology-enhanced plans, gain a better understanding of the human issues in the application of technology, and learn how technology can be applied to their own professional practice through the creation of personal portable reference libraries and portfolio materials.

Regional Accrediting Organizations of Schools and Colleges

Middle States Association of Colleges and Schools
3624 Market ST
Philadelphia, PA 19104-2680
Phone: 215.662.5603
Facsimile: 215.662.0957
E-mail: info@css-msa.org
Web site: www.css-msa.org

New England Association of Schools and Colleges
209 Burlington RD, Suite 5
Bedford, MA 01730-1433
Phone: 781.271.0022
Facsimile: 781.271.0950
E-mail: kwillis@neasc.org
Web site: www.neasc.org

North Central Association of Colleges and Schools
Schools Section
Arizona State University
Farmer Building, Room 110
PO Box 873011
Tempe, AZ 85287-3011
Phone: 800.525.9517
E-mail: nca@nca.asu.edu
Web site: www.nca.asu.edu

Northwest Association of Schools and Colleges
Schools Section
Boise State University
1910 University DR
Boise, ID 83725
Phone: 208.334.3210
E-mail: pjarnold@cocnasc.org
Web site: www.cocnasc.org

Southern Association of Colleges and Schools
1866 Southern LN
Decatur, GA 30033-4097
Phone: 800.248.7701
Web site: www.sacs.org

Western Association of Schools and Colleges, Inc.
Corporate Headquarters
985 Atlantic AVE, Suite 100
Alameda, CA 94501
Phone: 510.748.9001
Fax: 510.748.9797
E-mail: wascsr@wascsenior.org
Web site: www.wascWeb.org

Accrediting Commission for Schools, WASC
E-mail: mail@acswasc.org
Web site: www.acswasc.org

Conclusion

E-books can be a resource to expand the collection of any school library or media center, whether by subscription, use of freely available books, or creation. E-book collections make books more accessible to students, not just by providing more titles and more copies, but by having built-in accommodations for students with special needs. Access to resources can also be expanded by placing e-books on the Internet, creating a presence that can serve students 24 hours a day, seven days a week. Imagine the wondrous possibilities afforded by having books that are always in the collection, can always be checked out, never have to be shelved, and never have to be returned.

Online Resources

E-book Conversion and Creation

Adobe Acrobat (e-book conversion site): www.gobcl.com/convert_pdf.asp

HTML: Netscape Communicator (e-book creation program): http://wp.netscape.com/download/prodinfonfs_1.html

MS Reader: E-bookexpress (e-book creation program): http://lit.e-bookexpress.com

MS Reader: Word Add-in (e-book creation program): www.microsoft.com/reader/developers/info/rmr.asp

Online Libraries

Baen Science Fiction: www.baen.com

Blackmask Online: www.blackmask.com

Services

AvantGo (service that allows the selection of Web sites to be downloaded to hand devices): www.avantgo.com

Software

NoteStar (online tool that allows students to do online research including note-taking, organization, and automatic citation): http://notestar.4teachers.org

TrackStar (online tool to organize and annotate Web sites): http://trackstar.4teachers.org

Subscription Services

Accessible Book Collection (special needs): www.accessiblebookcollection.org

Bookshare.org (special needs): www.bookshare.org

ebrary (library): www.ebrary.com/index.jsp

netLibrary (library): www.netlibrary.com/Gateway.aspx

OverDrive Digital Library Reserve (library): www.overdrive.com

Questia (library): www.questia.com

Reading A–Z (online subscription service for leveled books that you print out): www.readinga-z.com

References

International Reading Association (IRA). (1999). *Library and media center adequacy: A position statement.* Newark, DE: Author.

International Reading Association (IRA). (2000). *Providing books and other print materials for classroom and school libraries: A position statement.* Retrieved September 2004 from www.reading.org/downloads/positions/ps1039_libraries.pdf

International Society for Technology in Education (ISTE). (1998). *National educational technology standards for students.* Eugene, OR: Author. Also available online at http://cnets.iste.org/students/s_stands.html

International Society for Technology in Education (ISTE). (2000). *National educational technology standards for teachers.* Eugene, OR: Author. Also available online at http://cnets.iste.org/teachers/t_book.html

Conclusion

Fulfilling the Promise

" Don't judge a book by its cover. "

This book started with the phrase "a book is a book is a book," but by this point we should also state that "a book is a computer, is a handheld, is a file" and "a computer can be a book, a book collection, or a library."

In short, the look of the book has changed. Along with this change in books has come a change in students. Today's students, sometimes called millennials, are technology users who have grown up and come of age with the Internet and reading text from a screen (Figure C.1). They see technology like the Internet as something that has always been available to them, with free and ubiquitous information that they can access at any time (Patrick, 2004).

In many situations, today's students feel that the assignments given at school actually discourage them from using technology as much or as creatively as they would like (Levin & Arafeh, 2002). Integrating Internet and computer applications into reading activities can provide direction and effective integration of technology for student success. It was estimated in 2001 that there were more than 20,000 free electronic versions of books, or e-books, available online (Project Gutenberg 2001), and the book numbers have been growing ever since. The books are there; the time has come to start using them.

Using e-book technology doesn't have to be expensive. Most schools already have the computers and access necessary to integrate e-books into classrooms, computer labs, and media centers. Even purchasing devices to use with students may be cost effective. Consider that an inexpensive handheld device costs approximately $100, and the average price of paperbacks is $4 with an educators discount. This means that a teacher would break even

Figure C.1. Internet use by age.

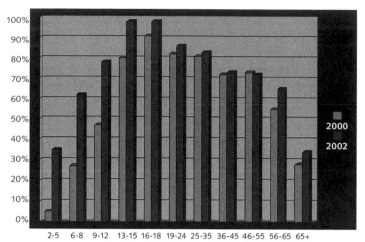

Source: NTIA (2004), U.S. Department of Commerce, using U.S. Census Bureau Current Population Survey Supplements.

by choosing to buy a handheld and after loading 25 free e-books. A sample compiled reading list was found to have more than 70 e-books currently available at no charge. When you also factor in the additional features of handheld devices, such as their ability to run educational software, access the Internet, act as calculators, and so forth, the advantages of choosing this route become even more clear. Combining the currently available technology with e-books provides not just a convenient and adjustable way to read, but a whole host of tools and resources for enhancing the reading experience. Think of the e-book device as a pocket bookshelf, with not only books, but other supporting tools for yourself and your students to use while reading and learning.

By now you should have a basic understanding of e-books, what they are, what they work with, and how to use them in an educational situation. If you have not yet done so, now is the time for you to read an e-book. Make sure that you first get comfortable and consider your ergonomic issues, such as having a good chair, using proper lighting, blinking often enough, and so on. One of the biggest complaints that I get about e-books is that people cannot lay in bed and read them, so I guess they don't have a handheld, because I read my e-books in bed, in the car, while watching TV (during the commercials), waiting in line, and in various other situations. Make sure you practice reading an e-book on a computer or laptop and also on a handheld device, if you have access to one. I suggest that you start your e-book experience by reading an electronic version of a book you've already enjoyed. You're going to be having new experiences and learning new things with the change in the reading medium, so don't make it harder on yourself by having both the book and the technology be new. Make sure to play with the options and features in the software. I'm a strong believer in play learning theory. If others ask what you're doing, tell them you're practicing with new "technological based reading scaffolding tools"—it sounds really impressive. But remember: no pressure. Just relax and have a good read.

References

Levin, D., and Arafeh, S. (2002). *The Digital Disconnect: The Widening Gap Between Internet-Savvy Students and Their Schools.* Electronic version retrieved October 2004 from Pew Internet and American Life Project site http://www.pewInternet.org/pdfs/PIP_Schools_Internet_Report.pdf

Patrick, S. (2004). *The Millennials.* Excerpted from a speech presented at the No Child Left Behind eLearning Summit, Orlando, Florida.

National Telecommunications and Information Administration. (2004). *Computer and Internet Use.* Retrieved October 2004 from http://www.ntia.doc.gov/

Project Gutenberg. (2001). *Project Gutenberg official home site.* Retrieved January 2005 from http://www.promo.net/pg/

Appendix A

E-book Formats List

This appendix presents an alphabetical listing of many of the extension codes used for files. The list is not exhaustive.

.aa audible audiobook format

.asp (ASP) active server pages, a framework for building dynamic HTML pages

.au digital audio format

.avi (AVI) Windows video format

.btf (BTF) Braille ready file for use with a refreshable Braille display or Braille embosser.

.doc (DOC) Microsoft Word document file

.ebo (EBO) MS Reader annotations file

.exe (EXE) an executable program file

.gif (GIF) image format designed for drawings

.htm/html (HTML) file written in hypertext markup language for Web browser reading

.jpg (JPEG) image format designed for photographs

.lit (LIT) Microsoft Reader format

.lwp (LWP) Lotus Word Pro file

.mov (MOV) QuickTime video

.mp3 (MP3) digital audio format

.mpg (MPEG) video format

.pdb (PDB) PalmDOC file

.pdf (PDF) Adobe Reader file

.php (PHP) an HTML-embedded scripting language for authoring Web pages

.pml (PML) Palm Markup Language

.png (PING) image format for photographs or drawings

.pps (PPS) PowerPoint show file

.ppt (PPT) PowerPoint presentation file

.prc (PRC) Palm e-book file

.ra Real Media video

.rb Rocket e-book and e-reader devices file

.rtf (RTF) rich text file readable by most word processors

.rwp (RWP) ReaderWorks project file

.seb (SEB) Franklin eBookman format

.swf (SWF) Macromedia Flash format

.tk3 (TK3) files read by the TK3 reader from Nightkitchen

.tr TomeRaider e-book files

.txt (TXT) plain text format

.wmv (WMV) Windows media format

.wpd (WPD) WordPerfect document

Appendix B

NETS for Students (NETS•S)

The National Educational Technology Standards for Students (NETS·S) are divided into six broad categories. Standards within each category are to be introduced, reinforced, and mastered by students. Teachers can use these standards as guidelines for planning technology-based activities in which students achieve success in learning, communication, and life skills.

1. **Basic operations and concepts**
   - Students demonstrate a sound understanding of the nature and operation of technology systems.
   - Students are proficient in the use of technology.

2. **Social, ethical, and human issues**
   - Students understand the ethical, cultural, and societal issues related to technology.
   - Students practice responsible use of technology systems, information, and software.
   - Students develop positive attitudes toward technology uses that support lifelong learning, collaboration, personal pursuits, and productivity.

3. **Technology productivity tools**
   - Students use technology tools to enhance learning, increase productivity, and promote creativity.
   - Students use productivity tools to collaborate in constructing technology-enhanced models, preparing publications, and producing other creative works.

4. **Technology communications tools**
   - Students use telecommunications to collaborate, publish, and interact with peers, experts, and other audiences.
   - Students use a variety of media and formats to communicate information and ideas effectively to multiple audiences.

5. **Technology research tools**
   - Students use technology to locate, evaluate, and collect information from a variety of sources.
   - Students use technology tools to process data and report results.
   - Students evaluate and select new information resources and technological innovations based on the appropriateness to specific tasks.

6. **Technology problem-solving and decision-making tools**

- Students use technology resources for solving problems and making informed decisions.

- Students employ technology in the development of strategies for solving problems in the real world.

Appendix C

NETS for Teachers (NETS•T)

All classroom teachers should be prepared to meet the following standards and performance indicators.

I. Technology Operations and Concepts

Teachers demonstrate a sound understanding of technology operations and concepts. Teachers:

A. demonstrate introductory knowledge, skills, and understanding of concepts related to technology (as described in the ISTE National Educational Technology Standards for Students).

B. demonstrate continual growth in technology knowledge and skills to stay abreast of current and emerging technologies.

II. Planning and Designing Learning Environments and Experiences

Teachers plan and design effective learning environments and experiences supported by technology. Teachers:

A. design developmentally appropriate learning opportunities that apply technology-enhanced instructional strategies to support the diverse needs of learners.

B. apply current research on teaching and learning with technology when planning learning environments and experiences.

C. identify and locate technology resources and evaluate them for accuracy and suitability.

D. plan for the management of technology resources within the context of learning activities.

E. plan strategies to manage student learning in a technology-enhanced environment.

III. Teaching, Learning, and the Curriculum

Teachers implement curriculum plans that include methods and strategies for applying technology to maximize student learning. Teachers:

A. facilitate technology-enhanced experiences that address content standards and student technology standards.

B. use technology to support learner-centered strategies that address the diverse needs of students.

C. apply technology to develop students' higher order skills and creativity.

D. manage student learning activities in a technology-enhanced environment.

IV. Assessment and Evaluation

Teachers apply technology to facilitate a variety of effective assessment and evaluation strategies. Teachers:

A. apply technology in assessing student learning of subject matter using a variety of assessment techniques.

B. use technology resources to collect and analyze data, interpret results, and communicate findings to improve instructional practice and maximize student learning.

C. apply multiple methods of evaluation to determine students' appropriate use of technology resources for learning, communication, and productivity.

V. Productivity and Professional Practice

Teachers use technology to enhance their productivity and professional practice. Teachers:

A. use technology resources to engage in ongoing professional development and lifelong learning.

B. continually evaluate and reflect on professional practice to make informed decisions regarding the use of technology in support of student learning.

C. apply technology to increase productivity.

D. use technology to communicate and collaborate with peers, parents, and the larger community in order to nurture student learning.

VI. Social, Ethical, Legal, and Human Issues

Teachers understand the social, ethical, legal, and human issues surrounding the use of technology in PK–12 schools and apply that understanding in practice. Teachers:

A. model and teach legal and ethical practice related to technology use.

B. apply technology resources to enable and empower learners with diverse backgrounds, characteristics, and abilities.

C. identify and use technology resources that affirm diversity.

D. promote safe and healthy use of technology resources.

E. facilitate equitable access to technology resources for all students.

Index